D0832419

Great Salvation Themes

by Dr. Jack Van Impe

JACK VAN IMPE MINISTRIES
Box J • Royal Oak, Michigan 48068

Printed in the United States of America

Second printing

Jack Van Impe Ministries
Box J, Royal Oak, Michigan 48068
In Canada: Box 1717, Postal Station A
Windsor, Ontario, N9A 6Y1
ISBN 0-934803-06-4

CONTENTS

Introduction

The Apostle Paul declared, *...I am not ashamed of the gospel of Christ: for it is the power of God unto salvation to every one that believeth* (Romans 1:16). Then, in 1 Corinthians 15:1-4, he added, *Moreover, brethren, I declare unto you the gospel...how that Christ died for our sins according to the scriptures; And that he was buried, and that he rose again the third day according to the scriptures.*

These two Bible passages clearly show that eternal life comes through believing and that salvation is in and through the Lord Jesus Christ—specifically His death, burial, and resurrection. Salvation, however, is more than simply believing in God and knowing the facts about Christ, for *...the devils also believe, and tremble* (James 2:19).

This book is a comprehensive investigation of the doctrine of salvation and the person and work of Christ. Its pages portray the great fundamentals of the faith—Jesus' deity, virgin birth, blood atonement, and bodily resurrection. It also reviews His last seven sayings upon the cross. Our study will prove that Jesus was indeed the Son of God (see Mark 15:39), yes, God in the flesh (see John 1:1-14), and that through the shedding of His blood He opened the way for mankind to be reconciled to God.

For the Christian, these great salvation themes will serve to confirm one's faith. For the unbeliever, they will convict of sin and foster faith, for *...the word of God is quick, and powerful, and sharper than any twoedged sword, piercing even to the dividing asunder of soul and spirit, and of the* joints and marrow, and is a discerner of the thoughts and intents of the heart (Hebrews 4:12).

If you have never placed your faith in Christ, receiving Him as your personal Lord and Saviour, I pray that this book will help you to do so. Remember, *Neither is there salvation in any other: for there is none other name under heaven given among men, whereby we must be saved* (Acts 4:12).

How shall we escape, if we neglect so great salvation (Hebrews 2:3).

—Dr. Jack Van Impe

Chapter 1

The Birth of the Eternal God

I feel that there is a tremendous need to enlighten mankind as to the true identity of Christ. Multitudes think of the Saviour as just another member of the human race born nearly 2,000 years ago. Nothing could be further from the truth. In this chapter I clearly want to trace the preexistence of Christ to prove that He was "the Eternal God" who became man in order that He might die for poor, helpless, hopeless sinners. I also want to show that His birth had to be through the channels of a virgin, inseminated by the power of the Holy Spirit, if His sacrifice for sinners was to be effective.

Christ's Preexistence

The altogether lovely One, born in Bethlehem's manger, existed from all eternity. The verse that prophesies His exact birthplace also tells of His preexistence. Micah 5:2: *But thou, Bethlehem Ephratah, though thou be little among the thousands of Judah, yet out of thee shall he come forth unto me that is to be ruler in Israel; whose goings forth have been from old, from everlasting.* Isaiah masterfully handles this truth in chapter 9, verse 6, *For unto us a child is born, unto us a son is given: and the government shall be upon his shoulder: and his name shall be called Wonderful, Coun-*

sellor, The mighty God, The everlasting Father, The Prince of Peace.

Let's analyze this verse for a moment. Notice that a *child is born* (this speaks of the Lord's birth), but the next phrase mentions a son being given. This speaks about God sending the Son who was in His presence and coincides with Galatians 4:4, *...when the fulness of the time was come, God sent forth his Son.* Then Isaiah goes on to proclaim this Son as God by the titles "The mighty God" and "The everlasting Father." These terms are possible because of the relationship of the Trinity. Remember that Jesus said in John 10:30, *I and my Father are one.*

John opens his gospel with the statement, *In the beginning was the Word, and the Word was with God, and the Word was God. The same was in the beginning with God. All things were made by him; and without him was not any thing made that was made* (John 1:1-3). In verse 14, he identifies this member of the Trinity who is called the "Word." *And the Word was made flesh, and dwelt among us.* Think of it. This One who was in the beginning with God and was God became flesh and lived among insignificant human beings because of His love for sinners.

Yes, Christ always existed and came from heaven to earth. Listen to His numerous statements verifying this truth: *For the bread of God is he which cometh down from heaven, and giveth life unto the world* (John 6:33). *I am the living bread which came down from heaven* (John 6:51). *Ye are from beneath; I am from above: ye are of this world; I am not of this world* (John 8:23). *I proceeded forth and came from God* (John 8:42). *I came forth from the Father, and am come into the world* (John 16:28).

In His high priestly prayer, Jesus said, *I have glorified thee on the earth: I have finished the work which thou gavest me to do. And now, O Father, glorify thou me with thine own self with the glory which I had with thee **before the world was*** (John 17:4,5). Jesus said in John 5:46, *Moses...wrote of me.* Here Christ delves back hundreds of years to the first five books of the Bible, called "The Pentateuch," and states that Moses mentioned Him. This is important because Moses recorded these words centuries before the birth of Christ. Jesus also said in John 8:56, *Your father Abraham rejoiced to see my day: and he saw it, and was glad.* How could Abraham see His day centuries before His birth if there were no preexistent One?

Oh, friend, Jesus always existed as a coequal member of the Trinity. Don't listen to a group of blinded cultists who would rob Christ of His deity, but hear the Word of the Lord. His preexistence is also proven through the Bible statements indicating that He created the world. John 1:3: *All things were made by him.* John 1:10: *He was in the world, and the world was made by him, and the world knew him not.* Colossians 1:16: *For by him were all things created, that are in heaven, and that are in earth, visible and invisible, whether they be thrones, or dominions, or principalities, or powers: all things were created by him, and for him.* Hebrews 1:2 states, *By whom* [Christ] *also he made the worlds.*

The part Christ had in creating the world and mankind agrees with the Old Testament account of creation. Genesis 1:1: *In the beginning God created the heaven and the earth.* The Hebrew for God is *Elohim*, a plural noun, meaning "more than one." This is a glorious declaration of the Trinity. You don't believe it? What will you do with Genesis 1:26? *And God said, Let us make man in our image, after our likeness.*

We have but skimmed the surface of evidence that proves that Christ preexisted His earthly birth. Now let's move on to the glorious truth of His coming to earth via the channel of a virgin's womb. At this point let's consider Philippians 2:5-8 because it is such a glorious transitional passage. It brings the eternal God from heaven to a bodily appearance upon earth so that He might die for sinners. *Let this mind be in you, which was also in Christ Jesus: Who, being in the form of God* [His spirit form in eternity], *thought it not robbery to be equal with God: But made himself of no reputation, and took upon him the form of a servant, and was made in the likeness of men* [His birth]. Why? Verse 8: *And being found in fashion as a man, he humbled himself, and became obedient unto death, even the death of the cross.*

Christ's Virgin Birth

Lost religionists mock the virgin birth. In an issue of the magazine *Challenge*, a number of sickening articles and poems appeared. I quote one of them to show the world how far liberal modernistic religionists will go in their attempt to rob Christ of His deity. It is a poem about Mary, the mother of Jesus. In the poem she says:

First, I've got nothing to say—about anything that happened before Joseph and I got married. Jesus was our child. Joseph's and mine. You can believe it or not. Suit yourself. He was my first born so naturally I thought he was something special. So, he's the Messiah they say. I'd rather he had stayed a carpenter, married a nice Jewish girl and given me a lot of fat little grandchildren.

What blasphemy! This is the prophecy of the Apostle Peter fulfilled before our eyes. *But there were false prophets also among the people, even as there shall be false teachers among you, who privily shall bring in damnable heresies, even denying the Lord that bought them, and bring upon themselves swift destruction. And many shall follow their pernicious ways; by reason of whom the way of truth shall be evil spoken of* (2 Peter 2:1,2).

Yes, the way of truth is often evil spoken of because of ordained wolves in sheep's clothing who call themselves members of the "Christian faith" and yet would tear Christ to shreds if the opportunity presented itself. The crucifixion would be mild in comparison to what some of our lost seminary professors would do to Jesus if they had the chance in this twentieth century. However, let's not waste our time on man's drivel but instead invest it wisely as we listen to the Word of God concerning the truth about the virgin birth.

A virgin birth was necessary because Adam sinned. Since Adam was the head of the human race, every person born into it through natural generation or through the process of birth inherits the old sinful Adamic nature. Romans 5:12: *Wherefore, as by one man* [Adam] *sin entered into the world, and death by sin; and so death passed upon all men, for that all have sinned.* Yes, all sinned or became guilty of sin simply by inheriting the fallen nature of Adam at birth. Quirks and diseases are passed on from generation to generation. Sugar diabetes is a prime example. Likewise, the sin nature is passed on to every generation. Romans 5:18 is another verse that clearly teaches the necessity of a virgin birth. *Therefore as by the offence of one* [Adam] *judgment came upon all men to condemnation; even so by the righteousness of one* [Christ] *the free gift came upon all men unto justification of life.*

Notice that judgment came upon all men unto condemnation because of Adam's sin, but through the righteousness of Christ one may be liberated from this judgment. It is only logical to conclude that if Christ had come through the normal channels of reproduction, He would have also been born with this judgment of condemnation upon Him because He also would have inherited Adam's sinful nature. Therefore, in order that He might set men free from this condemnation, He had to be born in another manner so as not to be tainted with the old wicked nature of Adam.

The Birth of the Eternal God

There was only one way this possibility existed and that was through a virgin birth—bypassing man through insemination of the virgin's ova by the Holy Spirit. This ova lies dormant in every woman until it is activated by a male sperm. Gasoline is also dormant until activated by a spark. Is it an impossibility for the God, who formed man out of the dust of the ground and took a rib out of man to form woman, to place the activating seed within this holy virgin and bring forth His Son through the miracle working power of His Holy Spirit? Of course not. This is exactly what the Father did. Hear the Word of God.

The very first messianic prophecy is found in Genesis 3:15. There we hear the Lord God uttering a prophecy against the serpent, saying, *And I will put enmity between thee and the woman, and between thy seed and her seed; it* [the woman's seed] *shall bruise thy head, and thou shalt bruise his heel.* The statement, "her seed," is the first reference to the virgin birth in God's Word. All humans are from the seed of man, but the seed of a woman implies a stupendous miracle. Jeremiah 31:22 again speaks of a miraculous event that would occur upon this earth, *...for the Lord hath created a new thing in the earth, A woman shall compass a man.*

A woman conceiving and bearing a man-child would not be a new thing in the earth—this is the rule of life. After conception takes place one bears a male or female child. Therefore this entirely new thing that would transpire had to be a miracle. What was it? A woman, without any human intervention or penetration, would conceive, carry, and deliver a man-child. This happened to be the the Lord Jesus Christ, Saviour of the world. Isaiah 7:14 again sheds light on this event of the ages. *Therefore the Lord himself shall give you a sign; Behold, a virgin shall conceive, and bear a son, and shall call his name Immanuel.* Isaiah is not merely referring to a young woman giving birth to a son. That would not be a sign. Millions of young women have been able to bear sons. The sign is that a virgin shall bear a son without an act of intercourse.

Forget the arguments of the religious contortionists who argue that the Hebrew word *almah* is "young woman" instead of "virgin." All one need do is study Matthew 1:23 where the Greek word *parthenos* can only be translated "virgin" to arrive at a final answer. *Behold, a virgin shall be with child, and shall bring forth a son, and they shall call his name Emmanuel, which being interpreted is, God with us.* Verse 22 states that this is a quotation from the prophet. What prophet? Isaiah. And where did Isaiah make the statement? Chapter 7, verse 14. So, the Greek text handles the Old Testament Hebrew text proving that God meant a "virgin" and not a "young woman."

I repeat what was stated earlier: A young woman bearing a child would be no sign. Any of you young expectant mothers reading this would be the first to realize this truth. However, had you become impregnated miraculously by the power of God without knowing a man, it would very obviously be a sign. That happened to Mary and only to Mary.

The reason that God the Son, originally in spirit form (see Philippians 2:5), had to have an earthly birth is found in Hebrews 10:4,5). *For it is not possible that the blood of bulls and of goats should take away sins. Wherefore when he cometh into the world, he saith, Sacrifice and offering thou wouldest not* [animal blood could not take away sin], *but a body hast thou prepared me.* Since animal blood only covered sin and was presented as a down payment for sin's debt until God's Lamb should come, Christ had a body with divine blood prepared in the womb of a virgin so that He could shed that blood and die for the sins of the world. Because it had to be pure blood, free from the taint of Adam's sin, the body and blood were prepared by the Father and placed in the womb of the virgin Mary.

Luke 1:26-34 depicts this thrilling story: *And in the sixth month the angel Gabriel was sent from God unto a city of Galilee, named Nazareth, To a virgin espoused to a man whose name was Joseph, of the house of David; and the virgin's name was Mary. And the angel came in unto her, and said, Hail, thou that art highly favoured, the Lord is with thee: blessed art thou among women.... And the angel said unto her, Fear not, Mary: for thou hast found favour with God. And, behold, thou shalt conceive in thy womb, and bring forth a son, and shalt call his name JESUS.... Then said Mary unto the angel, How shall this be, seeing I know not a man?*

This is a precious truth. Though she was espoused or engaged to Joseph, she had not known a man or experienced premarital sex. Remember that God wrote the Bible, and He declares that Mary was a pure virgin. Away with the mentally warped, religious hypocrites who are so defiled that they imagine all sorts of depraved things about this sweet virgin. Not everyone thinks and acts as they do. Mary declares, "I have never known a man— how shall this baby be conceived?" The blessed answer is found in verse 35: *The Holy Ghost shall come upon thee, and the power of the Highest shall overshadow thee: therefore also that holy thing which shall be born of thee shall be called the Son of God.* Anyone who believes that God created this gigantic, fantastic, and astronomical universe certainly believes that God can bring His only begotten Son into the world by a separate act of creation. *...with God nothing shall be impossible* (Luke 1:37).

There is the entire story. The preexistent God, second member of the Trinity, came to take upon himself a body with blood so as to shed His blood for sinners. The sin-tainted blood inherited from Adam would not qualify Him as the sinless Saviour, so a body was prepared with blood, produced by the Father, and placed into the womb of a virgin by the blessed Holy Spirit. Christ eventually went to the cross and shed His blood. Because He was the God-man shedding untainted holy blood, mankind may have eternal life by receiving this sacrifice. You have listened to false religious instructors long enough. Believe the Word of God—see Christ crucified and risen again. Receive this Christ today.

Chapter 2

The Deity of Christ

The thought of an eternal God being born may seem to be a contradiction of terms, but when one studies the God-man, the Lord Jesus Christ, insurmountable evidence supporting this truth manifests itself upon the pages of Holy Writ. The teachings of Christ's deity must be an accepted truth if one is to enter the eternal home of the redeemed.

John, in his first epistle, makes this dogmatic assertion: *That which was from the beginning, which we have heard, which we have seen with our eyes, which we have looked upon, and our hands have handled, of the Word of life; (For the life was manifested, and we have seen it, and bear witness, and shew unto you that eternal life, which was with the Father, and was manifested unto us)* (1 John 1:1,2). There is no doubt that the One John saw, heard, and touched was that Eternal Life which was with the Father.

In chapter 2, verse 22 of this same epistle, John goes on to say, *Who is a liar but he that denieth...the Father and the Son.* When one denies that Christ is the eternal One who came to earth clothed in human flesh, this skeptic or doubter immediately is classified as a liar and an antichrist. Since no liar or antichrist may enter the presence of God in that condition, it is abundantly clear that the one who denies the eternity of Christ is lost.

In 1 John 4:1-3 another warning is presented. *Beloved, believe not every spirit, but try the spirits whether they are of God: because many false prophets are gone out into the world.* How does one recognize the false prophets? Verse 2 and 3: *Hereby know ye the Spirit of God: Every spirit that confesseth that Jesus Christ is come in the flesh is of God: And every spirit that confesseth not that Jesus Christ is come in the flesh is not of God: and this is that spirit of antichrist.* Since *spirits* refers to teachers or preachers, the apostle is saying that preachers denying the doctrine of God coming in the flesh are preachers or teachers possessed by the spirit of Antichrist. God wrote it. I only quote it, but I believe it.

Then John states in chapter 5, verse 1, *Whosoever believeth that Jesus is the Christ is born of God. Messiah,* translated *Christus* or *Christ* means "the Sent One." Since He was sent from the Father, the conclusive proof is that He already existed. If He preexisted His mission to earth, He did not begin in Bethlehem's manger. The teaching of the Holy Bible is that He eternally existed as God, the second member of the Trinity, and came to earth to be clothed with a body containing blood so that He might die for sinners. Is He really God? Did He really exist before His birth upon earth? What does the Holy Spirit state in the Word of God?

Christ's Deity in the Old Testament

Isaiah 9:6 states, *For unto us a child is born, unto us a son is given: and the government shall be upon his shoulder.* This prophet speaks about Christ's incarnation and humanity in the phrase *a child is born* and about His eternity and deity in the other phrase *a son is given.* Incarnation comes from the Latin words *in* and *carnis* meaning "flesh" or "in the flesh." Thus, at this incarnation or coming in the flesh, He was the child born. However, as the son given, He always existed—uncreated and unborn.

Micah 5:2 states, *Whose* [His] *goings forth have been from of old, from everlasting.* This again points to the uncreated, eternal Son of God. Psalm 45:6: *Thy throne, O God, is for ever and ever: the sceptre of thy kingdom is a right sceptre.* This great Old Testament scripture, addressed to God, is about the Lord Jesus Christ. Who said so? The greatest authority in heaven and earth—Jehovah, the Father. Prove it? I will!

In Hebrews 1:8 we find Jehovah God of the Old Testament speaking: *...unto the Son he saith, Thy throne, O God, is for ever and ever: a sceptre of righteousness is the sceptre of thy kingdom.* Isn't this fantastic? The Father calls Christ "God" for ever and ever. Followers of Jehovah would be wise to listen to His voice and give Christ the glory due His holy name. God had His Son with Him from all eternity past. Christ was present when the human race was created. The Father, Son, and Holy Spirit were involved in Genesis 1:26 when God said, *Let us make man in our image, after our likeness.* The pronouns *us* and *our* speak of a plurality or trinity of personages. This same Christ was present when the earth was formed and set into motion. Proverbs

30:4: *Who hath ascended up into heaven, or descended? who hath gathered the wind in his fists? who hath bound the waters in a garment? who hath established all the ends of the earth? what is his name, and what is his son's name, if thou canst tell?* The Son is present in the Old Testament scriptures hundreds of years before His human birth occurs in the New Testament. Rational, logical contemplation makes one realize that He preexisted as God, the Son.

Christ's Deity in the New Testament (The Trinity)

The title of "God" is given to our Saviour on numerous occasions. Matthew 1:23 declares, *Behold, a virgin shall be with child, and shall bring forth a son, and they shall call his name Emmanuel, which being interpreted is, God with us.* In the first chapter of John, Christ is called "the Word." Verse 14: *And the Word was made flesh, and dwelt among us.* The only member of the Trinity who became flesh was Christ. Since the term *Word* is synonymous with *Christ*, as has just been proven, let's put the term *Christ* in place of *Word* in John 1:1-3 and see the results. *In the beginning was Christ, and Christ was with God, and Christ was God. The same was in the beginning with God. All things were made by Christ; and without Christ was not any thing made that was made.*

John 1:10 states, *He* [Christ] *was in the world, and the world was made by him, and the world knew him not.* Now we have just heard from the

Author of this book, the Holy Spirit, who said that Christ was from the beginning, that He was God, and that He created the world. Yes, Christ shared this creative ministry with the Father and Holy Spirit. This is so because all three members of the one Godhead always existed.

To prove that the Holy Spirit was also present at the time of creation, one need only study Genesis 1:1,2. *In the beginning God* [this is the plural noun *Elohim*, meaning "more than one"] *created the heaven and the earth. And the earth was without form, and void; and darkness was upon the face of the deep. And the Spirit of God moved upon the face of the waters.* The combining of John 1:10 and Genesis 1:1,2 proves conclusively that the entire Trinity was present at the creation of the world.

Some scoff at the teaching of a Trinity. They say, "The word *Trinity* is not found in the Bible, so there can't be such a doctrine." Well, the word *Bible* is not found in the Bible either, but I guarantee that there is such a book—and the teaching of the Trinity is found repeatedly throughout God's Word. Man has given the title "Trinity" to the doctrine because the meaning of the word is "three." Since there are three—Father, Son, and Holy Spirit—"Trinity" is a properly designated theological term.

Let's continue our search of the Scriptures concerning the deity of Christ. The Philippian jailor cried out in Acts 16:30, *Sirs, what must I do to be saved?* Paul and Silas replied, *Believe on the Lord Jesus Christ, and thou shalt be saved, and thy house* (verse 31). The entire family made a commitment to this Christ and verse 34 finds them rejoicing. Why? Because they believed in God with all their house. Here is unequivocal proof that Christ is God. Compare the two verses again. Acts 16:31: *Believe on the Lord Jesus Christ, and thou shalt be saved, and thy house.* Verse 34 says he believed in God—the Christ of verse 31.

Again we see the truth in Romans 9:5 which states, *Christ came, who is over all, God blessed for ever.* First Timothy 3:16 declares, *...great is the mystery of godliness: God was manifest in the flesh...*, and Hebrews 1:8 says, *But unto the Son he saith, Thy throne, O God, is for ever and ever.* This is Jehovah God telling the world that His Son is God. Never mind the book peddlers who run from door to door with their teaching of Christ being an inferior God, a little created God. Some even call Him Michael, the archangel. Jehovah knows everything for He is omniscient and all-wise, and He calls Jesus "God." I say with Paul in Romans 3:4, *...let God be true, but every man a liar.*

Christ's Deity Through a Comparison of Old and New Testament Texts

Perhaps the most interesting and exciting proof of Christ's deity is discovered when one compares the statements of God in the Old Testament with His revealed truth in the New. For example, in Isaiah 42:8, God states, *I am the Lord: that is my name: and my glory will I not give to another, neither my praise to graven images.* Since Jehovah will not give His glory to another but is willing to share it with Christ, it is only logically deductible to say that they must be one and coequal. The sharing of this glory takes place when God's people lay their crowns at the feet of the Saviour in Revelation 4:10,11, saying, *Thou art worthy, O Lord, to receive glory and honour and power: for thou hast created all things, and for thy pleasure they are and were created.*

Again the King of glory is Jehovah in Psalm 24:10. *Who is this King of glory? The LORD of hosts, he is the King of glory.* The noun *LORD* in this text is the Hebrew word *Jehovah*, the name of the Father. However, when one examines 1 Corinthians 2:8, he discovers that the Lord of glory was crucified. Thus Christ is also called the Lord of glory. Will you Bible manipulators tell me how there can be two Lords of glory, coequal, if there is no Trinity?

Once again Isaiah 9:6 calls the child born and the son given, *The mighty God, The everlasting Father.* If these are titles of the Son, how many mighty Gods and everlasting Fathers are there? The answer is one because of the unity and oneness of the Trinity. Jesus said, *I and my Father are one* (John 10:30). Psalm 10:16 says, *The Lord* [Jehovah] *is King for ever and ever.* Again we have problems if there is no Trinity because we now have two kings. When one studies Revelation 19:11-16, he finds that Christ, the King of kings, comes to set up His Kingdom upon this earth. *And I saw heaven opened, and behold a white horse; and he that sat upon him was called Faithful and True.* Verse 16: *And he hath on his vesture and on his thigh a name written, KING OF KINGS, AND LORD OF LORDS.*

This constant reiteration of identical names and titles for both Father and Son can mean only one thing to honest searching hearts. It is that Christ is God, coequal with the Father and Holy Spirit. Deuteronomy 32:39 states, *There is no God* [but Jehovah] and yet 1 Timothy 3:16 tells us that *God* [came] *in the flesh.* The only solution is the doctrine of the Triune God which the saints of all ages have proclaimed. The only groups in the annals of history that ever fought this precious truth were rebel-rousing heretics.

Mr. Scoffer, you who would make Christ but a mere man, what will you do with Jonah 2:9? *Salvation is of the Lord.* Or Isaiah 43:11 which says, *I, even I, am the Lord* [Jehovah]; *and beside me there is no saviour.* If there is no other Saviour but Jehovah and Christ is called "the Saviour" scores of times in the Bible, then He and the Father must be one or there are two Saviours. Christ is the God who left the bosom of the Father to die on Calvary's cross. There He shed the pure sinless blood that coursed through His veins so that sinners might be eternally saved. The Bible teaches that He is the only Saviour. Acts 4:12: *Neither is there salvation in any other: for there is none other name under heaven given among men, whereby we must be saved.* Since both Jehovah and Christ are called "Saviour," let's believe that the Trinity alone presents the answer.

Christ Was Incarnated, Not Created

There are those who teach that the Father always existed and that Christ was created. Perish the thought! Christ always existed and was not created. Isaiah 43:10 states, *...before me there was no God formed, neither shall there be after me.* In simple English, no God was created before or after Jehovah. They coexisted as a Trinity eternally. Thus Christ was from all eternity or He wasn't. Either He always existed or He didn't. Since no God was created before or after Jehovah, we take Micah 5:2 for what it says about the One who was to come to earth and experience a human birth. He was *from of old, from everlasting.* Thus, His human birth was not His creation. Rather, as we discussed earlier in this chapter, the word *incarnation* comes from the Latin words *in* and *carnis* meaning "in the flesh."

An eternal God having a birth is not contradictory. In eternity He was God. To become a man, a birth had to occur. None of us can become another species without the miracle of a birth. God had to become incarnated (become flesh) so that He could shed the pure, sinless blood that flowed in His veins. The miracle of the Holy Spirit's insemination of the virgin Mary's ova and womb with the body and blood of God the Son made this shedding of blood possible. This was a necessity because the blood of animals could not take away sin, only cover the sinner's transgression.

Hebrews 10:4 states, *For it is not possible that the blood of bulls and of goats should take away sins.* So, verse 5 has Christ saying, *A body hast thou prepared me.* God lived in that body, went to the cross in that body, shed the blood in that body to take away the sins that had only been covered, died in that body, arose three days later in that same body, ascended to heaven in that body, and will throughout eternity live in that body in which He had the birth. *For in him dwelleth all the fulness of the Godhead bodily* (Colossians 2:9).

There it is. The eternal God left heaven to be born into human flesh because a body could contain sinless blood through a virgin birth. That blood was shed for sins and can wash you from every stain and taint of this world's defilement when you put your trust in the God in whom the Philippian jailor trusted, the Lord Jesus Christ. Do it today.

Chapter 3

The Purpose of the Incarnation

The past two chapters dealt with the preexistence of Christ, His deity, and His incarnation. This chapter will thoroughly cover the reason that the eternal God had a birth date into our world.

An Eternal Plan

Why did God come through the channel of a virgin's womb? Why was it necessary for God, in spirit form, to take upon himself a body? Philippians 2:5-8 explicitly explains this great theological truth. *Let this mind be in you, which was also in Christ Jesus: Who, being in the form of God, thought it not robbery to be equal with God: But made himself of no reputation, and took upon him the form of a servant, and was made in the likeness of men: And being found in fashion as a man, he humbled himself, and became obedient unto death, even the death of the cross.*

The phrase, *He humbled himself, and became obedient unto death, even the death of the cross* is the focal point of this discussion. God the Father, God the Son, and God the Holy Spirit held a meeting in eternity past and planned the entire program of redemption. All three were at that time in spirit form. God the Father was and still is a spirit (see John 4:24). The Holy Spirit was and still is a spirit (see John 16:13). Christ was a spirit because He was (past tense) in the form of God, which we have already proven to be a spirit form (see Philippians 2:6).

However, at this meeting of the Trinity in ages past, it was agreed that one of the three would eventually become a human with a covering of flesh, and Christ was the elected member to fulfill salvation's plan. This can all be proven from the Holy Scriptures. First Peter 1:20: *Who* [Christ] *verily...was manifest in these last times for you. Messiah* means "sent one." If He is the Sent One, He did not originate at Bethlehem's manger. Instead, Galatians 4:4,5 pictures the facts as they occurred. *But when the fulness of the time was come, God sent forth his Son, made of a woman, made under the law, To redeem them that were under the law....*

Does this simplistic doctrinal truth penetrate your reasoning processes? Hear it again. *God sent forth his Son, made of a woman.* There it is— Christ's deity and humanity, His eternity and birth. God sent the Son who was in His presence, meaning that Christ existed as God before coming to earth. However, He was *made of a woman* when He was sent. This is, of course, the virgin birth which took place in the manger centuries ago when God became man.

When the Trinity outlined the plan, all the events of future history were foreknown. Remember, God knows everything. The plan progressed according to the omniscience of the Godhead. Since God knows everything about everything and all things about all things, the following points were known thousands, yes, millions of years before they occurred:

1. **Man's disobedience and fall.**

God placed man in the garden of Eden with certain restrictions. Genesis 2:17: *But of the tree of the knowledge of good and evil, thou shalt not eat of it: for in the day that thou eatest thereof thou shalt surely die.* The slithering serpent came along and said in Genesis 3:4, *Ye shall not surely die.* Instead of listening to Jehovah God, Adam and Eve listened to the devil.

Say, all of us are so much like them. We certainly are chips off the old block. Genesis 3:6 states, *And when the woman saw that the tree was good for food, and that it was pleasant to the eyes, and a tree to be desired to make one wise, she took of the fruit thereof, and did eat, and gave also unto her husband with her; and he did eat.* This wicked, disobedient act against the Lord God Almighty brought judgment upon the entire human race. *For as by one man's disobedience many were made sinners, so by the obedience of one* [Christ] *shall many be made righteous* (Romans 5:19).

Not only did God foreknow the fall of man, but:

2. **The Trinity foreordained the temporary sacrifice.**

I imagine the conversation in the heavenlies went as follows: "Because man will yield to temptation and fall, there will need to be a sacrifice offered. Since sinful flesh is responsible and since *the life of the flesh is in the blood* (Leviticus 17:11), the decree is established in the counsels of eternity that the shedding of blood, which typified DEATH to the flesh, will be the eternal sacrifice offered. *It is the blood that maketh an atonement for the soul* (Leviticus 17:11). Animal blood will be temporarily offered until one of us goes to present the permanent sacrifice." Let's investigate the facts and see if God's program was instituted.

After Adam and Eve sinned they knew that they were naked (see Genesis 3:7). The pangs of a guilt-ridden conscience over sin were being experienced. They wanted to cover their bodies and did so by making fig leaf aprons. However, fig leaves that would shrivel up and die in a few days could not satisfactorily handle the situation. Also, dry fig leaves were bloodless and could not make an atonement for the soul. So God, in the cool of the day, visited this couple and covered them adequately—physically and spiritually. *Unto Adam also and to his wife did the Lord God make coats of skins, and clothed them* (Genesis 3:21). The skins of animals adequately covered them physically and spiritually. Why? In providing the skins, the blood of the animals was shed.

We see the same story unfolded in Genesis 4 concerning Cain and Abel. Their parents, Adam and Eve, had taught them this soul-saving story about the animal skins. Now when the boys were of age and wanted to bring a sacrifice to God, Cain presented an offering of fruit and Abel, of animals. Genesis 4:3-5: *And in process of time it came to pass, that Cain brought of the fruit of the ground an offering unto the Lord. And Abel, he also brought of the firstlings of his flock and of the fat thereof. And the Lord had respect unto Abel and to his offering: But unto Cain and to his offering he had not respect.*

If you should think that I am stretching the point by stating dogmatically that Cain's offering was rejected because it was devoid of blood, I invite you to confirm this truth in your heart by studying Hebrews 11:4 which emphatically presents the teaching just considered. *By faith Abel offered unto God a more excellent* [more acceptable] *sacrifice than Cain.*

Notice they brought their offerings as a sacrifice. God had decreed that blood alone could make an atonement for the soul. Abel by faith brought an animal. Notice why he did it. It was by faith. Romans 10:17 says, *So then faith cometh by hearing.* If he brought it by faith and faith comes by hearing, it is only a logical conclusion to say that he heard the story from the lips of his parents, accepted it, and practiced the shedding of blood because he believed God. Cain, the first liberal or modernist, said, "It's all bunk. I will offer my fruit which contains no blood, and God will have to be satisfied." But God said, "Cain, I reject your bloodless sacrifice."

Many have rejected the only method of salvation God has given the world—the shedding or sacrifice of blood for the remission of sins. Self-righteous efforts, good works, prayers, creeds, and religious observances are but offerings of fruit. The Sermon on the Mount, the Golden Rule, and the observance of the Ten Commandments are but the waving of fig leaves in the face of Almighty God. Many of these things are good to practice because one is a Christian, but any method of trying to enter into eternal life that avoids or bypasses the blood will only result in eternal separation from the God who made the decree. *It is the blood that maketh an atonement for the soul* (Leviticus 17:11). Now, let's go one step farther.

3. **The Trinity foreordained the permanent eternal sacrifice.**

Again we hear the three members of the Godhead speaking in eternity past: "Animal blood will be only a temporary solution because it cannot take away sin, only cover it. Man's blood is tainted through Adam's sin. Therefore only one option or course of action is possible. One of the three of us will have to go to earth and take flesh as a covering. This will be necessary because flesh contains the blood of the body. The One who is chosen to go will have to shed that blood to take away the sins of the human race which animal blood only covered.

"The One who goes and takes upon himself that body must have a special birth, because all humans born through natural generation or through the regular channels of birth inherit the old wicked sinful nature of Adam. Therefore, the One chosen will have to have a special birth in the womb of a virgin. The very body will be created and placed in that womb. By this special act of creation—detouring the normal means of reproduction through intercourse—the Saviour will be born into the world. When His blood, holy and pure, is shed, it will take away sin."

The Eternal Truth

Does this conversation of the Trinity in ages past seem farfetched to you? Are you wondering if this entire plan presented is really in the Bible? Listen to Revelation 13:8, [Christ was]...*the Lamb slain from the foundation of the world.* When? In God's mind it was planned at the time of the foundation of the world. That's right, even before Adam and Eve were created. Christ's shedding of His blood did not take Him by surprise nearly 2,000 years ago. Rather, it was part of the plan He had helped initiate before the world was formed. That's why Acts 2:23 states, *Him* [Christ] *being delivered by the determinate counsel and foreknowledge of God, ye have taken, and by wicked hands have crucified and slain.* In other words, the wicked only did to Christ what the foreknowledge of God had planned.

Did it happen? Yes. God came into the world in human flesh to take a body that contained blood. It was special blood that did not have the taint of Adam's sin integrated into it by Christ's having a human father. Instead, the Father and the Holy Spirit placed this created miracle into the womb of the virgin without an act of intercourse or human insemination so that pure blood might course through the Redeemer's veins. Then He shed that blood at Calvary to take away sin that had only been covered by animal sacrifices.

The proof of these truths is in the following scripture. Hebrews 10:4: *For it is not possible that the blood of bulls and of goats should take away sins.* Notice, animal blood could not take away sins. The Old Testament word *atonement* means "to cover"— only "to cover." The priest offering the animal blood would say, "I know that this blood only covers the sinner's sin until your sacrificial Lamb comes, dear God."

Who was God's Lamb? Hebrews 10:5: *Wherefore* [because animal blood could not take away sin] *when he cometh into the world, he saith, Sacrifice and offering thou wouldest not, but a body hast thou prepared me.* That body was prepared in the womb by God the Father and God the Holy Spirit. Luke 1:35: *And the angel answered and said unto her, The Holy Ghost shall come upon thee, and the power of the Highest shall overshadow thee: therefore also that holy thing which shall be born of thee shall be called the Son of God.*

When John the Baptist saw Christ upon the earth he said in John 1:29, *Behold the Lamb of God, which taketh away the sin of the world.* Praise God, this was the Lamb sent from heaven who could take away that which was only temporarily covered through the blood of animals. On the cross, Christ cried out, "It is finished." He was not speaking about His life, but about the plan that had been foreordained before the foundation of the world. Am I certain of this? Yes. [We have been] *redeemed...with the precious blood of Christ, as of a lamb without blemish and without spot: Who verily was foreordained before the foundation of the world* (1 Peter 1:18-20).

The Purpose of the Incarnation

Imagine, this precious blood shed for your sins was planned for you before the world was formed. Seven hundred times the blood is mentioned as the only—THE ONLY—way of salvation. Believe it and receive the Christ who shed that pure blood for your transgressions.

Chapter 4

The Lord Jesus Christ: Saviour of the World

The Holy Bible gives God's Son manifold titles. However, the one that means so much to all of us as poor, helpless sinners is "Saviour"—which immediately instills hope within one's heart concerning salvation. The very name *Jesus* means "salvation." Matthew 1:21 states, *...thou shalt call his name JESUS: for he shall save his people from their sins.* Multitudes today are trusting in man-made rituals to get them inside God's heaven. Yet, there isn't a ceremonial rite in all of Christendom's churches that can save a man. Jesus Christ alone is the only way to eternal life.

Christ's Saving Power

Mary the mother of Jesus in that tremendous portion of Scripture often described as the "Magnificat," cried out, *My soul doth magnify the Lord, And my spirit hath rejoiced in God my Saviour* (Luke 1:46,47). In Luke 2, the angel of the Lord appeared to the shepherds, saying, *...behold, I bring you good tidings of great joy, which shall be to all people. For unto you is born this day in the city of David a Saviour, which is Christ the Lord* (verses 10,11).

Also in Luke 2, Simeon had been waiting for the consolation or hope of Israel. He jubilantly exclaimed, *Lord, now lettest thou thy servant depart in peace, according to thy word: For mine eyes have seen thy salvation* (verses 29,30). He was looking upon the Christ child as he spoke those words.

Again in John 4, a wicked woman—who had five husbands and who was living under common law with number six—turned to Jesus Christ for forgiveness. Then she excitedly ran back to the city and told the people about her newfound joy in this Saviour who had blotted out her sordid past. The men of that city listened to the Lord's discourses for two days and exuberantly stated, *Now we believe, not because of thy saying: for we have heard him ourselves, and know that this is indeed the Christ, the Saviour of the world* (verse 42).

In Acts 5, Peter and some of the apostles were threatened with punishment, even unto death (verse 33). However, the great Apostle Peter so loved Jesus. He believed so strongly in the fact that Jesus was the only way of salvation and eternal life that he was willing to die in order that the message might be proclaimed. I can almost hear this impulsive preacher saying, *We ought to obey God rather than men. The God of our fathers raised up Jesus, whom ye slew and hanged on a tree. Him hath God exalted with his right hand to be a Prince and a Saviour...* (verses 29-31).

Acts 13:23 calls Him *a Saviour, Jesus.* Ephesians 5:23 says, *Christ is the head of the church: and he is the saviour of the body.* Compare this verse with 1 Corinthians 12:13, *For by one Spirit are we all baptized into one body....* The body of

Christ, into which one is implanted at the time of regeneration, is the Church, and Ephesians 5:23 states that Christ is the Saviour of this body. Baptism, reformation, confirmation, works, creeds, and human efforts cannot place one into the true Church because only the Lord Jesus Christ is the Saviour of this body. Amen!

The Apostle Paul stated that one of the reasons he was willing to endure suffering, torture, and even death was because of his trust in the Saviour. Death could only mean that the One who saved him would welcome him home to heaven. Hear him in 1 Timothy 4:10. *For therefore we both labour and suffer reproach, because we trust in the living God, who is the Saviour of all men, specially of those that believe.*

In 2 Timothy 1:9 and 10, Paul went on to say that it was not a system of self-attainment through works that would place him eternally in the glory land, but rather a precious Saviour whose name was Jesus Christ. Listen to the simplicity of these instructive verses. [God] *hath saved us, and called us with an holy calling, not according to our works, but according to his own purpose and grace, which was given us in Christ Jesus before the world began, But is now made manifest by the appearing of our Saviour Jesus Christ, who hath abolished death, and hath brought life and immortality to light through the gospel* [or through the good news].

Again, He *hath abolished death.* What wonderful words! *And* [He] *hath brought life and immortality to light through the gospel.* Immortality

39

speaks of eternal life—and it comes through the gospel or the "good news." Do you get the impact? Eternal life is through the gospel and *gospel* means "good news."

This good news is explained in 1 Corinthians 15:1-4 where we find that Christ died, was buried, and rose again the third day according to the Scriptures. Put it all together and it simply says that everlasting life does not come through one's denominational record or good works. It comes as a result of one's acceptance of the Saviour's death by the shedding of blood and of His resurrection. Titus 2:13 speaks of Christ's return by stating, *Looking for that blessed hope, and the glorious appearing of the great God and our Saviour Jesus Christ.* Notice that it is not Buddha, Mohammed, or Zoroaster who is the Saviour, but only the Lord Jesus Christ. There is no other Saviour—Jesus is the only way. Second Peter 1:1 again calls Him *...our Saviour Jesus Christ.*

Christ's Earthly Ministry

"Saviour" is not some honorary title which was bestowed upon the Lord Jesus Christ in recognition of His wonderful teachings. Rather, it depicts His ministry upon earth and speaks of His saving power.

Presently, we are living in a time of rebellion. Corrupted mankind is trying to destroy all of our foundational structures. This trend can also be witnessed in the religious world as apostate, liberal clergymen mock the doctrines of the virgin birth, the deity of Christ, His blood atonement upon the cross, and His bodily resurrection. Many laugh at the statement "Jesus Saves" as if the word "saves" were an invention of some simpleton.

Our God predicted this would happen, and it is one of the signs of the end. Second Peter 2:1,2: *But there were false prophets also among the people, even as there shall be* [one of the signs] *false teachers among you, who privily shall bring in damnable heresies, even denying the Lord that bought them, and bring upon themselves swift destruction. And many shall follow their pernicious ways; by reason of whom the way of truth shall be evil spoken of.*

There are two things one can do for these poor misguided souls; (1) pray for them, and (2) thank God for their presence because it means that Jesus Christ is coming soon to call Christians home. Let them laugh. The term *saved* was placed in the Bible scores of times by a Holy God. One had better investigate and accept this truth if he is interested in eternal life.

I could quote numerous verses proving that salvation is of God and that God put this word in the Bible. However, let's limit our discussion to those which speak exclusively about Christ being the way of salvation: *Thou shalt call his name JESUS: for he shall save his people from their sins* (Matthew 1:21). *For the Son of man is come to save that which was lost* (Matthew 18:11). *God sent not his Son into the world to condemn the world; but that the world through him* [Jesus] *might be saved* (John 3:17).

41

Jesus said, *I am the door: by me if any man enter in, he shall be saved...* (John 10:9). *I came not to judge the world, but to save the world* (John 12:47).

Paul said, *Believe on the Lord Jesus Christ, and thou shalt be saved...* (Acts 16:31). *For I am not ashamed of the gospel of Christ* [not rites, ceremonies, rituals, the Sermon on the Mount, the Golden Rule, or the Ten Commandments, but the gospel or the good news of Christ]: *for it is the power of God unto salvation to every one that believeth...* (Romans 1:16). *We shall be saved from wrath through him* (Romans 5:9). *If thou shalt confess with thy mouth the Lord Jesus, and shalt believe in thine heart that God hath raised him from the dead, thou shalt be saved* (Romans 10:9).

In 1 Corinthians 15:1,2 we find this statement, *Moreover, brethren, I declare unto you the gospel* [the good news] *which I preached unto you, which also ye have received, and wherein ye stand; By which also ye are saved....* How? Verses 3 and 4: *Christ died for our sins according to the scriptures; And...he was buried, and...he rose again the third day according to the scriptures.* This alone is the message of the gospel, the good news, the only way of salvation. Christ died, shed His blood, and rose again.

Christ's Redeeming Blood

Christ's power to save all the world was wrought through His precious blood shed on Calvary. Leviticus 17:11: *It is the blood that maketh an atone-*

ment for the soul. Acts 20:28: ...the church of God, which he hath purchased with his own blood. First Peter 1:18,19: Forasmuch as ye know that ye were not redeemed with corruptible things, as silver and gold, from your vain conversation received by tradition from your fathers; But with the precious blood of Christ, as of a lamb without blemish and without spot. Revelation 1:5: Unto him that loved us, and washed us from our sins in his own blood. Yes, ...without [the] shedding of blood [there] is no remission [of sins]... (Hebrews 9:22).

It is not enough simply to state that Christ died— as so many intellectuals do today in order to do away with the sacrifice of His blood. A bloodless death on the cross would not have saved anyone. Let me repeat that. Had Christ died of a heart attack or of suffocation upon the cross, mankind would have been lost forever, for it is the blood that maketh an atonement for the soul. Because of this fact, Christ came to earth to take upon himself a body with blood so that He might shed that blood for our sins (see Hebrews 10:5). When one receives this sacrifice of the shed blood of Jesus Christ, he is saved immediately.

Christ's Redemptive Purpose

If the Lord Jesus Christ is the Saviour and has saving power, we may conclude that He came to earth because sinners need saving. This is exactly what Paul said, This is a faithful saying, and worthy of all acceptation, that Christ Jesus came into the world to save sinners... (1 Timothy 1:15). Not only does this statement include everyone we know, but ourselves as well. Christ would have all men to be saved, including you and me (see 2 Timothy 2:4). [Christ] gave himself a ransom for all... (1 Timothy 2:6).

The only reason some people will never get saved is that they do not realize that they are lost. They think they were born into sainthood just like the Pharisee in the temple. He said, I thank thee, that I am not as other men are... (Luke 18:11). However, Jesus said in Matthew 5:20, Except your righteousness shall exceed the righteousness of the scribes and Pharisees, ye shall in no case enter into the kingdom of heaven.

Why? The Pharisees were so caught up in the admiration of their own goodness that they were convinced they needed nothing from God—nothing at all! Yet, God says in Isaiah 64:6, We are all as an unclean thing, and all our righteousnesses are as filthy rags.... Galatians 3:22: The scripture hath concluded all under sin.... Thus, God not only wants to save mankind from the misery of sin in this life, but also from the eternal penalty into which sin will drag those who reject Christ. He that believeth not the Son shall not see life; but the wrath of God abideth [eternity] on him (John 3:36). Why? Because he won't receive the Son.

Oh, my friend, if you are lost, the Saviour longs to save you. You need saving because all are sinners and only through His blood can you be washed white. You may be whitewashed because you've had all the rituals of the Church performed upon you, but you really need to be washed white to inherit eternal life! Why not call on Him right now, saying, "Lord Jesus, come into my heart."

Chapter 5

The Supreme Sacrifice
of the Lord Jesus Christ

The world will never know a sacrifice greater than that made by the Lord Jesus Christ in paying the price of mankind's redemption. He willingly relinquished His claim to the attributes and possessions to which He was fully entitled as God. By investigating Christ's sacrifice in detail, one immediately begins to appreciate the Saviour's work on his behalf.

The Apostle Paul beautifully told the story in Philippians 2:5-8. *Let this mind be in you, which was also in Christ Jesus: Who, being in the form of God, thought it not robbery to be equal with God: But made himself of no reputation, and took upon him the form of a servant, and was made in the likeness of men: And being found in fashion as a man, he humbled himself, and became obedient unto death, even the death of the cross.* Again in 2 Corinthians 8:9 we find, *For ye know the grace of our Lord Jesus Christ, that, though he was rich, yet for your sakes he became poor, that ye through his poverty might be rich.*

Christ's Heavenly Home

First of all, the Lord Jesus sacrificed His heavenly home. Heaven is a place where joy, happiness, and pleasure abound. The psalmist, speaking to his God in Psalm 16:11, said, *...in thy presence is fulness of joy; at thy right hand there are pleasures for evermore.* In heaven there is no fear of being mugged, robbed, or raped, because the wicked are not there to make trouble, *and there the weary be at rest* (Job 3:17).

Christ the Saviour came from that heaven to give His life and blood to save sinners. He said, *I am the living bread which came down from heaven...* (John 6:51). Jesus so loved sinners that He left the palatial mansions of His home above to become a poverty-stricken pauper, if I may use that terminology reverently.

During His sojourn upon earth, Jesus had no home and few possessions. In Matthew 8, a scribe flippantly told the Lord that he wanted to follow Him. Immediately Christ informed him of the cost involved, saying, *The foxes have holes* [a place into which they crawl at night for sleep], *and the birds of the air have nests; but the Son of man* [Jesus] *hath not where to lay his head* (verse 20). No home —not even His own bed. Oh, our Lord had so little as He walked this earth.

Christ's Honor

Secondly, the Lord Jesus sacrificed His honor. I do not mean by this statement that He did wrong, because [He] *did no sin* (1 Peter 2:22). [He] *knew no sin* (2 Corinthians 5:21). Christ is *...holy, harmless, undefiled,* [and] *separate from sinners* (Hebrews 7:26).

Instead, my thought is that the world dishonored Him. Psalm 22 is messianic, meaning that it is all about the Lord Jesus Christ in prophetical form. Prophetically, we hear Jesus saying the following, beginning with verse 6, *I am a worm, and no man; a reproach of men, and despised of the people. All they that see me laugh me to scorn: they shoot out the lip, they shake the head....*

Verses 11-15: *...there is none to help. Many bulls have compassed me: strong bulls of Bashan have beset me round. They gaped upon me with their mouths, as a ravening and a roaring lion. I am poured out like water, and all my bones are out of joint: my heart is like wax; it is melted in the midst of my bowels. My strength is dried up like a potsherd; and my tongue cleaveth to my jaws; and thou hast brought me into the dust of death.* Verse 17: *I may tell all my bones: they look and stare upon me.* Oh, when one considers these verses, his soul should cry out, "Lord Jesus, I love You. If ever I loved You, my Saviour, it's now."

Was Christ ridiculed and hated? Did these predictions materialize? You be the judge. The "religious" Pharisees said, *This fellow doth not cast out devils, but by Beelzebub the prince of the devils* (Matthew 12:24). The scribes claimed, *He hath an unclean spirit* (Mark 3:30). Again, the Pharisees said, *We be not born of fornication* [sexual impurity]... (John 8:41). They even mocked the precious virgin birth as so many apostate preachers do today. If you have done this, you ought to repent, turn to Christ, and experience real Christianity.

The Pharisees also said, *This man is not of God, because he keepeth not the sabbath day...* (John 9:16). The Pharisees again said to the man whose blindness was healed by Jesus, *Give God the praise: we know that this man* [Jesus] *is a sinner* (John 9:24). Imagine! They called Jesus "a sinner." However, the man replied, *Whether he be a sinner or no, I know not: one thing I know, that, whereas I was blind, now I see* (John 9:25).

Oh, friend, so many yet today are blind as to who Jesus really is. He is the Saviour of the world—the only Saviour. They could have their eyes opened if only they would give Him a chance and receive Him. Still, they refuse to believe, just like the scribes and Pharisees who said, *He hath a devil, and is mad* [demented and out of His mind] (John 10:20). *For a good work we stone thee not; but for blasphemy; and because that thou, being a man, makest thyself God* (John 10:33).

Reflect a moment on these slanderous accusations. They called Jesus the prince of the devils. They claimed He had an unclean spirit (see Mark 3:30). They said He was one born of sexual impurity, one who kept not the Sabbath, one who was a sinner, one who had a devil, one who was mad and demented, one who was a blasphemer. Yet this One of whom they spoke was the Lord Jesus Christ—God in the flesh. Oh, when He came to die, He certainly sacrificed His honor.

Why did Jesus Christ, the Lord of glory, allow all of this? Philippians 2:6-8 again tells the story. *Who, being in the form of God* [before He came to earth],...*made himself of no reputation....* How?

[By taking] *upon him the form of a servant...made in the likeness of men.* Why? Verse 8: *And being found in fashion as a man, he humbled himself, and became obedient unto death, even the death of the cross.*

Christ's Sacrificial Love

Perhaps the most unfathomable aspect of Christ's sacrifice is the fact that His love chose this lifestyle. He wanted to sacrifice His all to save us. Yes, He became poor that we, dear friend, might become rich. The way one can become rich is to partake of the eternal life He provided as He shed His blood on Calvary's cross. When one has life—abundant, eternal life—he has the wealth of all of the international bankers combined. They will die after 70 years and leave it behind. The Christian's wealth, however, will abide forever.

Have you claimed this eternal life by receiving Jesus Christ? The Bible says in John 3:36, *He that believeth on the Son hath everlasting life....* Jesus said in John 6:47, *Verily, verily, I say unto you, He that believeth on me hath everlasting life.*

Christ's Efficacious Blood

The fourth and most important possession sacrificed by Christ was His life through the shedding of His blood. This sacrifice must be continually emphasized in a day and age when the bloodshed of Christ upon a cross has become insignificant. This fact must be reiterated thousands of times when unbelieving clergymen scoff at the message of His precious blood, calling it a "slaughterhouse religion."

How pathetic that ministers can be so blind as to preach a system of man-made works to get sinners into heaven. Laymen who make cookies for the bake sale and sell old socks at the church rummage bazaar in order to work their way into heaven also need to know that the old Book, God's Word, contains 700 verses pointing to the shed blood as God's offering and only—ONLY—plan of salvation.

Titus 3:5: *Not by works of righteousness which we have done, but according to his mercy he saved us, by the washing of regeneration....* This washing is through Christ's blood as Revelation 1:5 declares, *Unto him that loved us, and washed us from our sins in his own blood.* The sacrifice which wrought salvation brought great agony and suffering to the body and soul of Jesus Christ our Lord. Just before He was crucified, He said, *My soul is exceedingly sorrowful, even unto death* (Matthew 26:38). Hebrews 12:2 states, *Looking unto Jesus the author and finisher of our faith.*

I like that. Jesus is the Author and Finisher—or the Originator and Consummater—of our faith. Our salvation is not based on works, creeds, ceremonies, prayers, or a code of ethics, but in Christ. The text goes on to say, *...who for* [or because of] *the joy that was set before him endured the cross, despising the shame, and is set down at the right hand of the throne of God.* In modern English, we would say, "Because He could see what His shed blood on the cross was going to accomplish—the

Christian's presence with Him for all eternity—
Christ was willing to endure the suffering of being
nailed to the tree."

Christ also suffered for us... (1 Peter 2:21).
Christ...suffered for sins, the just [Jesus] *for the
unjust* [you and me], *that he might bring us to God,
being put to death in the flesh, but quickened* [or
made alive] *by the Spirit* (1 Peter 3:18). Observe the
suffering Saviour in Isaiah 53:4-6. *Surely he hath
borne our griefs, and carried our sorrows: yet we
did esteem him stricken, smitten of God, and
afflicted. But he was wounded for our transgressions, he was bruised for our iniquities: the chastisement of our peace was upon him; and with his
stripes we are healed. All we like sheep have gone
astray; we have turned every one to his own way;
and the LORD hath laid on him* [Jesus] *the iniquity of us all.*

This wounding and bruising took place so that
Christ's blood might flow freely for the remission of
sin. Envision for a moment Jesus on the cross of
Calvary. A crown of thorns is on His head, and the
blood is flowing down His cheeks into His beard.
His body has been lacerated by blows with sticks
and fists, and the blood flows from these wounds as
well. Portions of His beard have literally been ripped
from his face. In Isaiah 50:6, Christ in prophetical
utterance cries, *I gave my back to the smiters, and
my cheeks to them that plucked off the hair....* Can
you visualize it? Do you see Him? His chest, arms,
and back are torn wide open as a result of the
Roman scourge. Do you see the nails in His hands

and feet? *He was wounded for our transgressions, he was bruised for our iniquities.*

Christ's body was bruised horribly, terribly, almost beyond recognition. That's why Isaiah said in chapter 53, verse 2, *...he hath no form nor comeliness....* All of this was for the sin of mankind. There is no other way to be saved but through Christ's shed blood.

Acts 20:28 mentions *the church of God, which he hath purchased with his own blood.* The *true* Church has been purchased by Christ's blood, and your church is swindling you if it offers a stone of self-righteous human attainment—the dry vegetable offering or religion of Cain, the murderer (see Genesis 4). First Peter 1:18,19 states that we are *redeemed...with the precious blood of Christ.* First John 1:7: *...the blood of Jesus Christ His* [God's] *Son cleanseth us from all sin.* Ephesians 1:7: *In whom we have redemption through his blood....* Only the sacrifice of Christ's blood can save. Had Jesus died of strangulation or heart failure upon the cross, we could not be saved, because *...without shedding of blood* [there] *is no remission* [of sin] (Hebrews 9:22).

If you are sincerely seeking the truth, quit listening to bloodless, pompous platitudes from the pulpit. They can only mislead you on earth and will make you miss being in the presence of God for eternity. If some lost clergyman has deceived you into thinking that the shed blood for salvation is passé in the twentieth century, then hear Christ himself. The scene is the Last Supper, and Jesus illustrates through bread and juice His coming sacrifice upon the cross. Matthew 26:26-28: *And as they were eating, Jesus took bread, and blessed it, and brake it, and gave it to the disciples, and said, Take, eat; this is my body. And he took the cup, and gave thanks, and gave it to them, saying, Drink ye all of it; For this is my blood of the new testament, which is shed for many for the remission of sins.*

There is no mistaking or denying it. Christ's *blood* was shed for the remission of sin. If you reject this truth because some ordained wolf in sheep's clothing has told you that such talk is passé for modern Christians, I can only have sorrow for his condition and yours. Why? Because both of you have listened to man rather than Jesus Christ, the Saviour. Hear Him, believe Him. His shed blood is the only way of salvation.

Chapter 6

The Lord Jesus Christ:
The Only Way of Salvation

Salvation is not found in man-made ceremonies. Neither is it obtained through ordinances or religious sacraments. Instead, *Salvation is of the Lord* (Jonah 2:9). Still, multitudes believe that the pursuance of good works or the following of a prescribed code of ethics automatically earns them the guarantee of eternal life. Others talk about the benefits of the Golden Rule, the Sermon on the Mount, or the observance of the Decalogue—God's Ten Commandments—as the way to prepare one's soul for heaven. Although such ideals should be part of a believer's life, they are a *result* of salvation, not a means of achieving it.

Ephesians 2:10 states, *For we are his workmanship, created in Christ Jesus unto good works....* In other words, good works accompany salvation because Christ, who lives within the believer, is doing the work in him. Thus, we see that it is because one is saved that he works. He does not work in order to become saved. Too often, however, mankind puts the cart before the horse and attempts to reverse the gears of God's program. The result is humans trying to do that which only Almighty God can do. The end is frustration, false doctrine, and eternal damnation. Man plays no part in obtaining salvation. It is all of God. Titus 3:5 declares, *Not by works of righteousness which we have done, but according to his mercy he saved us, by the washing of regeneration, and renewing of the Holy Ghost.*

God's Word

Let me be as dogmatic as I have ever been and state that our Holy God has provided no other way of salvation except through the merits of the shed blood of the Lord Jesus Christ. *Neither is there salvation in any other: for there is none other name under heaven given among men, whereby we must be saved* (Acts 4:12). Notice that last phrase again—*There is none other name under heaven given among men, whereby we must be saved.* Buddha, Mohammed, Confucius, Zoroaster, Dr. Moon, Maharajah Ji, and multitudes of others are unable to save because the Holy Word of God explicitly states that there is no other name or god who can save. Christ is the *only* Saviour.

Someone may immediately and antagonistically cry out within himself, *He is quoting some isolated text from Scripture. The Bible is not that narrow in its limitations concerning salvation. Were he using all of the Scriptures, his conclusion would be different.* Let me tell you something shocking. I read the entire New Testament through in a four-day period, marking every verse indicating that salvation is in Christ alone, not in creeds, works, ethics, rites, or ceremonies. I found approximately 400 portions of Scripture presenting this clear-cut truth.

Now if God said it once, that would satisfy my searching mind. However, when He declares it nearly 400 times, one had better believe it. In fact, I am presenting the entire list later in this chapter. The heart of every believer in the Lord Jesus Christ will be blessed as he takes time to study each of these passages. For the present, let's examine just a few of the texts which prove that only Christ can bring salvation to needy hearts. We will begin with the statements of the Saviour himself.

Jesus' Word

In order to bombard you with truth, my comments on the verses will be limited. This way I can cover approximately 75 portions of God's Word.

Matthew 16:18: *...upon this rock I will build my church....*

Matthew 26:28: *...this is my blood of the new testament, which is shed for many for the remission of sins.*

Mark 8:38: *Whosoever therefore shall be ashamed of me and of my words in this adulterous and sinful generation; of him also shall the Son of man be ashamed, when he cometh in the glory of his Father with the holy angels.*

In Luke 5:24, Christ states that *...the Son of man hath power upon earth to forgive sins.*

Luke 19:10: *...the Son of man is come to seek and to save that which was lost.*

To the thief on the cross, the Saviour said, *To day shalt thou be with me in paradise* (Luke 23:43). Only God could make such a promise.

In John 4:13,14, the Lord said to the woman at the well, *Whosoever drinketh of this water shall thirst again: But whosoever drinketh of the water that I shall give him shall never thirst; but the water that I shall give him shall be in him a well of water springing up into everlasting life.*

In John 5:40, Christ said, *...ye will not come to me, that ye might have life.*

John 6:37: *...him that cometh to me I will in no wise cast out.*

John 8:12: *...I am the light of the world: he that followeth me shall not walk in darkness, but shall have the light of life.*

John 8:24: *...if ye believe not that I am he, ye shall die in your sins.*

John 10:9: *I am the door: by me if any man enter in, he shall be saved....*

John 10:28: *...I give unto them eternal life....*

John 11:25: *...I am the resurrection, and the life.... Verse 26: ...whosoever liveth and believeth in me shall never die....*

John 12:32,33: *...if I be lifted up from the earth, [I] will draw all men unto me. This he said, signifying what death he should die.*

After hearing the statements of our Lord and Saviour Jesus Christ, one would do well to obey God the Father who said in Luke 9:35, *This is my beloved Son: hear him.*

Jesus also said in Matthew 12:30, *He that is not with me is against me....* One cannot say, "Oh, I admire Christ, but I believe there are other ways." One is either for Christ or against Him. One either accepts what Christ stated about himself through

35 pronouns and references or rejects it. Neutral one cannot be!

The Holy Spirit's Word

Next, let's consider the blessed Holy Spirit's statements, dictated as He moved upon the various Bible writers (see 2 Peter 1:20,21). Thus, we will actually be hearing from Him as we investigate the verses He inspired these men to write. I am using only that portion of each verse which supports the truth that salvation is found in Christ alone. Please investigate each one thoroughly, as nothing has been taken out of context.

Romans 1:16: *For I am not ashamed of the gospel of Christ: for it is the power of God unto salvation to every one that believeth....* Notice it is the good news concerning Christ that is the power of God unto salvation to all who believe. It is not to all who are sprinkled as babies or immersed as adults. It is not through confirmation or reformation. It is not based on works or a system of ethics such as the Sermon on the Mount, the Golden Rule, or the Ten Commandments. No, it is the good news about Christ that is the power of God unto salvation to all who—watch that word believe—*believe.*

Romans 5:1: *...we have peace with God through our Lord Jesus Christ.*

Romans 5:8: *...Christ died for us.*

Romans 5:9: *...we shall be saved from wrath through him.*

Romans 6:23: *...the gift of God is eternal life through Jesus Christ our Lord.*

Romans 8:1: *There is therefore now no condemnation to them which are in Christ Jesus....* Think of it—no judgment or hell if one is in Christ Jesus!

Romans 10:13: *For whosoever shall call upon the name of the Lord shall be saved.*

Romans 13:14: *...put ye on the Lord Jesus Christ....*

First Corinthians 1:2: [We are] *sanctified in Christ Jesus....*

First Corinthians 2:2: *For I determined not to know any thing among you, save Jesus Christ, and him crucified.* Why, Paul? He is the only way.

First Corinthians 3:11: *For other foundation can no man lay than that is laid, which is Jesus Christ.* He is the foundation on which the superstructure, the Church, has been built. Praise God, He is the rock or foundation, not Peter or any other man.

First Corinthians 6:11: *...ye are washed...in the name of the Lord Jesus....*

Second Corinthians 5:17: *Therefore if any man be in Christ, he is a new creature....*

Second Corinthians 12:2: *I knew a man in Christ....* Amen, that's the only way to be—in Christ.

Galatians 1:4: [Christ] *gave himself for our sins....*

Galatians 2:16: *Knowing that a man is not justified by the works of the law, but by the faith of Jesus Christ....*

Galatians 3:13: *Christ hath redeemed us from the curse of the law, being made a curse for us: for it is written, Cursed is every one that hangeth on a tree.*

Galatians 3:26: *For ye are all the children of God by faith in Christ Jesus.*

Galatians 5:1: *...Christ hath made us free....*

Ephesians 1:3: *...our Lord Jesus Christ, who hath blessed us with all spiritual blessings in heavenly places in Christ.*

Ephesians 3:17: *That Christ may dwell in your hearts by faith....*

Philippians 3:10: *That I may know him, and the power of his resurrection....*

Philippians 4:21: *Salute every saint in Christ Jesus....* Saints are produced in Christ.

Colossians 1:20: [He] *made peace through the blood of his cross....*

Colossians 1:27: *Christ in you, the hope of glory.*

Colossians 2:10: *...ye are complete in him....*

First Thessalonians 1:10: *...Jesus, which delivered us from the wrath to come.*

First Timothy 2:6: [Christ] *gave himself a ransom for all....*

Second Timothy 2:10: *...they may also obtain the salvation which is in Christ Jesus with eternal glory.*

Hebrews 2:9: *...that* [Christ] *by the grace of God should taste death for every man.*

Hebrews 5:9: *...he became the author of eternal salvation....*

Hebrews 10:12: *But this man* [Jesus], *after he had offered one sacrifice for sins for ever, sat down on the right hand of God.*

First Peter 2:24: *Who his own self bare our sins in his own body on the tree....*

Second Peter 2:20: *...they have escaped the pollutions of the world through the knowledge of the Lord and Saviour Jesus Christ....*

First John 4:9: *...God sent his only begotten Son into the world, that we might live through him.*

First John 4:10: [He] *sent his Son to be the propitiation of our sins.*

First John 5:11,12: *And this is the record, that God hath given to us eternal life, and this life is in his Son. He that hath the Son hath life; and he that hath not the Son of God hath not life.*

Jude 21: *...looking for the mercy of our Lord Jesus Christ unto eternal life.*

Revelation 5:9,10 pictures the eternal future when believers shall be with Christ in heaven. It also records the words of the song the redeemed shall sing in that day. *And they sung a new song, saying, Thou art worthy to take the book, and to open the seals thereof: for thou wast slain, and hast redeemed us to God by thy blood out of every kindred, and tongue, and people, and nation; And hast made us unto our God kings and priests: and we shall reign on the earth.* If one never sings about the blood of Christ in his high-class services, he will never find himself in heaven with the throngs singing redemption's story.

Revelation 7:14 pictures the Tribulation Hour. Here we find that the same plan of salvation exists after the Church is removed from this earth. *These are they which came out of great tribulation, and have washed their robes, and made them white in the blood of the Lamb.* Christ is the Lamb of God (see John 1:29).

Revelation 14:13 states that the only ones called blessed or happy are the dead which die in the Lord. If one doesn't die in the Lord, he will be lost. Dear reader, I sum it all up by saying that you will never see God unless you come by the way of Christ's shed blood upon the cross.

Revelation 21:27: *And there shall in no wise enter into it* [heaven] *any thing that defileth, neither whatsoever worketh abomination, or maketh a lie: but* [hear it, don't miss it] *they which are written in the Lamb's book of life* [Christ's book of life].

These references but skim the surface. Four hundred passages reiterate this same glorious truth. The following compilation of references from Matthew through Revelation is printed chronologically. This allows one to follow the entire program of verses by simply turning the pages of the New Testament. In fact, I suggest that you highlight or underline each portion in your own Bible as a permanent record. The list is by no means exhaustive. Try to find others in your own study of the Word.

Matthew
    7:21,22,23
    11:28,29,30
    16:18
    18:6
    19:14
    26:28
    27, 28 Gospel Story

Mark
  5:6
  8:35
  8:38
  9:41,42
  10:28,29,30,31
  15, 16 Gospel Story
Luke
  1:46,47
  2:11,29,30
  5:24,32
  9:23,24,25,26
  13:25
  19:10
  23:43
  23, 24 Gospel Story
John
  1:4,12,29
  3:16,17,18,36
  4:14,42
  5:40
  6:28,29,37,47,48,51
  7:5
  8:12,24
  9:38
  10:9,28
  11:25,26
  12:32,33
  14:6
  17:3
  19, 20 Gospel Story
  20:30,31

Acts
  1:8
  4:12
  5:30,31,42
  8:5,12,35,37
  9:20,27
  10:36,43
  13:38,39
  15:11,17
  16:30,31
  17:2,3,4
  20:21,28
  28:31
Romans
  1:16
  5:1,8,9,10,11,15,18,19,21
  6:23
  8:1,3,10,32,34,35,39
  9:33
  10:4,9,10,11,13
  12:5
  13:14
  14:10,11
  15:16,29
  16:18
1 Corinthians
  1:1,2,3,4,6,8,9,18
  2:2
  3:11
  4:1,10,15
  5:5
  6:11,15

10:4,16
11:1,25
15:1,2,3,4,23
16:22
2 Corinthians
2:12
4:4,5,6,14
5:15,17,18,19,21
8:9
10:7
11:2,10,23
12:2,19
13:5
Galatians
1:4,6,7,8,9 2:16,17,20
3:13,14,22,26,27,28,29
4:7
5:1,4,24
6:12,14,18
Ephesians
1:1,2,3,4,5,7,10,11,12,13,15,22,23
2:5,6,7,10,13,14,20,21
3:6,8,11,12,17
4:12,13,15,21,32
5:2,5,23,25,27,30
Philippians
1:1,6,27
2:10,11,16
3:8,9,10,14,18,20
4:13,19,21,23
Colossians
1:2,4,7,13,14,18,20,27,28
2:6,7,8,10

Great Salvation Themes

1 Peter
  1:18,19
  2:5,7,21,24
  3:18
  4:1
2 Peter
  1:1,11
  2:1,20
  3:18
1 John
  1:7,9
  2:2,24,25,28
  3:23
  4:9,10,14,15
  5:1,5,10,11,12,13,20
2 John
  1:9
Jude
  1:1,4,21,25
Revelation
  1:5,18
  3:20,21
  4:11
  5:9,10,12
  7:14
  12:11
  13:8
  14:4,13
  15:3
  19:1,9,10
  20:4
  21:7

At this point, one final question remains, "What will you do with Jesus?" You are a sinner. Christ shed His blood for your sin, and now you must receive Him. Remember the words to that old hymn:

"What will you do with Jesus?
   Neutral you cannot be;
Someday your heart will be asking,
   'What will He do with me?'"

If you reject Him, I can give you the answer today. John 5:40: *...ye will not come to me, that ye might have life.* Again, John 14:6: *No man cometh unto the Father, but by me.* Revelation 20:15: *And whosoever was not found written in the* [Lamb's] *book of life was cast into the lake of fire.*

Where will YOU spend eternity?

Chapter 7

The Lord Jesus Christ: The Sinner's Substitute

Thus far, we have discussed the Lord Jesus Christ as Saviour of the world and learned that He gave His own life by the shedding of blood to be that Saviour. Now we shall study our wonderful Lord as the substitute for helpless sinners.

Each of us is familiar with the term *substitute.* During our school days when the regular teacher became ill, another instructor filled his or her position. The replacement was called a "substitute" teacher. He was one who took the place of another. In theological studies, this principle is contained in the doctrine of the substitutionary or "vicarious" work of Christ. In other words, the Son of God, because of His enormous love for sinners, took our place or became our substitute.

Christ Bore Our Sin

In His substitutionary work, the Lord Jesus Christ took upon himself the sinner's sin. Oh, what love that a Holy God should leave heaven for earth's misery, in order that He might—in a body of flesh—take upon himself our sin. Yes, Jesus is God. *God was manifest in the flesh...* (1 Timothy 3:16). In Hebrews 1:8, the Father, speaking to His Son, says, *Thy throne, O God, is for ever and ever.* Jesus was in the form of God (a spirit) and came to earth to be made in the likeness of men (see Philippians 2:6,7). He did so in order that He might take the place of each sinner, thereby becoming the sinner's substitute.

As the God-man, He never experienced or tasted the dregs of sin because He was the Holy One. Isaiah was overwhelmed with the holiness of God, and he said in chapter 6, verse 3, *Holy, holy, holy, is the Lord of hosts: the whole earth is full of his glory.* Three times the prophet uttered that phrase—once for each member of the Trinity.

He continued in verse 5, *Woe is me! for I am undone; because I am a man of unclean lips, and I dwell in the midst of a people of unclean lips....* What made Isaiah feel so lowly? He had witnessed the holiness of God. The remainder of the verse tells. the story. *...for mine eyes have seen the King, the Lord of hosts.* I believe the One Isaiah saw was Jesus Christ because He is the One who bears the title, "KING OF KINGS."

In Revelation 19:11, the Lord Jesus Christ returns to earth, and the text states, *I saw heaven opened, and behold a white horse; and he that sat upon him was called Faithful and True....* Verse 13: *And he was clothed with a vesture dipped in blood* [this speaks of Christ's redemptive work as Saviour by the shedding of His blood]: *and his name is called The Word of God* [this ties in with His preexistence as expressed in John 1:1]. Then, in verse 16, we are presented with His glorious title: *And he hath on his vesture and on his thigh a name written, KING OF KINGS, AND LORD OF LORDS.*

Oh, dear friend, Jesus was, is, and always will be the Holy One. While upon earth He did no sin (see 1 Peter 2:22), He knew no sin (see 2 Corinthians 5:21), and He could victoriously challenge the crowds with the words, *Which of you convinceth me of sin?* (John 8:46).

The tremendous truth that I am about to present is that this totally holy, spotless Christ was willing to take mankind's filthy, vile, loathsome, abominable sin upon His being at Calvary. The Prophet Isaiah, so humbled as he beheld the King in His beauty and holiness, also saw Him bearing the degraded, depraved wickedness of all of earth's race. Thus, in chapter 53, verse 6, he said, *All we like sheep have gone astray; we have turned every one to his own way; and the Lord hath laid on him the iniquity of us all.*

This agrees with 2 Corinthians 5:21: *For he [Jehovah] hath made him [Christ] to be sin for us, who knew no sin; that we might be made the righteousness of God in him.* This is the good news—Christ died for our sins, was buried, and rose again the third day (see 1 Corinthians 15:3,4). *Who his own self bare our sins in his own body on the tree* (1 Peter 2:24). *Unto him that loved us, and washed us from our sins in his own blood* (Revelation 1:5).

Our Sin Grieved Christ

Can you imagine this Holy One bearing all the filth of the world at Calvary? This is what so deeply disturbed the Lord Jesus Christ in Gethsemane.

He knew He had come to shed His blood for sinners, for He planned it with the Father and Holy Spirit before the world was created. *Who verily was foreordained before the foundation of the world* (1 Peter 1:20). Jesus Christ is *...the Lamb slain from the foundation of the world* (Revelation 13:8). The crucifixion was not taking Him by surprise, for He had helped plan it.

His reason for crying out, *My soul is exceeding sorrowful, even unto death,* and *O my Father, if it be possible, let this cup pass from me* (Matthew 26:38,39), was His dreadful hatred of sin—my sin and your sin! The iniquity of all sinners, heaped upon Christ at His crucifixion, caused His Father to turn His face away from Him—forsaking Him during the hours that He was hanging upon that tree, bearing our wickedness.

Jesus knew that soon the cry of Matthew 27:46, *Eli, Eli, lama sabachthani* ("My God, my God, why has thou forsaken me?"), would become a reality. Just the thought of the weight of bearing all this sin was undeniably heavy for the Holy One who had never sinned. Nevertheless, He took our place and became our substitute. He bore our grief and sorrow as He filled our shoes. Isaiah 53:4 says, *Surely he hath borne our griefs, and carried our sorrows....*

Consider the extent of Christ's grief by meditating upon John 19:34: *But one of the soldiers with a spear pierced his side, and forthwith came there out blood and water.* Medical men at one time thought this to be an impossibility. The human body does not have enough water in that particular area to produce a flow. Through advanced science and technology in the medical field, today's doctors inform us that water may freely run from that area if an incision is made after one dies in grief. The supreme sacrifice made to save us, through the shedding of His blood, tormented and broke Christ's heart as revealed through the flowing of water from His side.

To bear every sinner's sin is an experience that none of us shall ever taste because Christ, the Holy One, has already endured it for us and was the only One who could. However, many of you know the torment of mind you are presently experiencing because of some hidden secret sin you are harboring. Multiply this billions of times or trillions of times and you will begin to comprehend just what Jesus experienced at Golgotha.

First Corinthians 6:9-11 lists just a few of the sins that Christ bore as He took our place: *Know ye not that the unrighteous shall not inherit the kingdom of God? Be not deceived: neither fornicators* [the sex sin between the unmarried], *nor idolaters, nor adulterers, nor effeminate, nor abusers of themselves with mankind* [homosexuals], *Nor thieves, nor covetous, nor drunkards, nor revilers, nor extortioners, shall inherit the kingdom of God.* Wait! The next verse says, *And such were some of you: but ye are washed, but ye are sanctified, but ye are justified in the name of the Lord Jesus....*

Christ, through His blood, can remove any and all sin if one will just call on Him. Read Romans 1:28-32 and Galatians 5:19-21 and discover that Christ also bore wickedness, maliciousness, envy, murder, deceit, backbiting, hatred of God, pride, disrespect for parents, uncleanness (or dirty, double-meaning jokes), lasciviousness, idolatry, witchcraft (which comes from the Greek word *pharmekeia* meaning "drug use"), hatred of others, strife and fighting, heresies, and drunkenness. Yes, He even died to save false, heretical teachers who deny the virgin birth, the deity of Christ, the blood atonement, and the bodily resurrection. The precious blood of the Lord Jesus Christ is so powerful and efficacious that nearly 2,000 years after it was shed, all these sins plus many others not mentioned will be immediately blotted out when one comes to Christ, for ...*the blood of Jesus Christ his* [God's] *Son cleanseth us from all sin* (1 John 1:7).

The total meaning of Christ's substitutionary sacrifice is best expressed in 2 Corinthians 5:21: *For he* [God] *hath made him* [Christ] *to be sin for us...that we might be made the righteousness of God in him.*

Christ Died Our Death

The Bible states, ...*the soul that sinneth, it shall die* (Ezekiel 18:4). *For the wages of sin is death...* (Romans 6:23). ...*sin, when it is finished, bringeth forth death* (James 1:15). This is not only referring to the first death (the grave), but also the "second death" which is the lake of fire (see Revelation 20:14,15).

There is no doubt about physical death being experienced by the Lord Jesus at the cross. Christ died that we might live. Yet, He said, ...*he that believeth in me, though he were dead, yet shall he live: And whosoever liveth and believeth in me shall never die...* (John 11:25,26). That which we call death today is but a transference into a richer, greater experience if one is born again. Philippians 1:21 states, *...to die is gain.* Why? For the Christian, to be absent from the body (that's what death is, a departure from the body) is to be present with the Lord (see 2 Corinthians 5:8).

What, then, is the "second death" or the lake of fire? It is a place of eternal suffering and separation from God. Not only did Jesus suffer physically at Calvary, He also suffered spiritually—being forsaken of God during His hours of agony. Because the vicarious or substitutionary sacrifice of Christ included the giving of His body and soul (physical and spiritual death), we see that the Lord Jesus Christ also bore the punishment of our second death (separation from the Father).

Yes, Jesus also suffered spiritually upon the cruel cross, for Isaiah 53:10 states, *...thou [Jehovah] shalt make his soul an offering for sin....* This means that during those excruciating hours on the cross, the Lord Jesus Christ bore in His soul every pang and pain our eternal judgment would have brought to us. Matthew 27:34 states, *They gave him vinegar to drink mingled with gall....* Notice that this took place twice—once before He was crucified (see Matthew 27:34) and again while He was dying upon the cross (verse 48). Gall was a pain killer. Verse 34 continues, *and when he had tasted thereof, he would not drink.* In effect, Christ was saying, "No, no, I've come to bear the sentence of death for the sinner in My body and in My soul, physically and spiritually, and I will bear every pang. Away with your narcotic pain killer."

As stated previously, the water which flowed from the Saviour's side indicated that tremendous grief was experienced as His body and soul were made an offering for sin. Surely all the fires of eternal hell surrounded Him as He hung upon the cross. No wonder He said, *My God, my God, why hast thou forsaken me?* (Matthew 27:46). Jehovah would have nothing to do with a place filled with sin, such as hell eventually becomes (see Revelation 20:11-15). Thus, when all the sins that will populate hell were laid upon Jesus Christ, the Father could not look at His Son until the sacrifice was completed. Praise God, when our Substitute finished His sacrifice, the Father approved and looked upon Him once again. That is the meaning of the resurrection (see Romans 4:25).

May I suggest that you read all of the accounts of the crucifixion story (Psalm 22, Isaiah 53, Matthew 27, Mark 15, Luke 23, and John 19) and then reread them. You will clearly see that the Lord Jesus Christ took both your first death and second death—the grave and the lake of fire—upon himself when He died. Because He took your place, bearing your sin and taking your penalty, you can receive forgiveness and eternal life simply by receiving what Christ did for you.

John 1:12: *...as many as received him, to them gave he power to become the sons of God....* When you receive Him, your judgment day will be past. [We are] *passed from death* [judgment or condemnation] *unto life* (John 5:24). Romans 8:1: *There is therefore now no condemnation to them which are in Christ Jesus....* Why? He paid the penalty for you. When you receive Christ, God says, [Your] *sins and iniquities will I remember no more* (Hebrews 8:12 and 10:17).

Potentially, your sin has been paid for by Christ through the cross. Experientially, you must receive what has been provided. Think of it! No sin, no judgment, and no hell. No sin because His blood can cleanse all from every stain and taint of the past. No judgment because His blood does such a thorough job of cleansing sinners that there's nothing left to judge. No hell because one whose sins have been washed away and whose sins cannot be found in God's book cannot be punished.

Praise the Lord! Your past can be liquidated, obliterated, and forgotten—and this will be your blessed experience today if you let Jesus Christ come into your life. If you reject Him, however, your sins will take you into the grave and then into the second death—the lake of fire—to be separated from the presence of God forever and forever and forever. Oh, be ready to meet Jesus Christ when the call to leave this world comes. Receive Him right now!

Chapter 8

Whitewashed or Washed White?

Everything a Christian is or can ever become is because of *...the precious blood of Christ...* (1 Peter 1:19). Now if this is so—and it is—what does Christ's blood accomplish and why is it called "precious"?

We Are Saved by the Blood

First, one is saved by the blood of Jesus. Have you ever heard a clergyman say, "The message of the cross is passé. Enlightened humanity no longer believes in such a primitive message. Doing one's best is all God requires, so forget the fanatic's ravings about Christ's blood. At best this is but a 'slaughterhouse' religion"?

Do you know why ministers make such blasphemous statements? The answer is found in 1 Corinthians 1:18, *...the preaching of the cross* [and the blood] *is to them that perish foolishness....* Now these Bible-rejecting perpetrators of error are literally *...enemies of the cross of Christ* (Philippians 3:18). They literally mock the language of God's Book which states, *...he* [was] *brought as a lamb to the slaughter...* (Isaiah 53:7), and *...it is the blood that maketh an atonement for the soul* (Leviticus 17:11).

Their bloodless religion proves that they are taking orders from another spirit, for 1 Timothy 4:1 declares, *Now the Spirit speaketh expressly, that in the latter times some shall depart from the faith, giving heed to seducing spirits, and doctrines of devils.* Say, neighbor, instead of listening to men, begin believing Christ! He, at the first communion service, said, *This is my blood of the new testament, which is shed for many for the remission of sins* (Matthew 26:28). Believe Him!

We Are Justified by the Blood

Second, a sinner is justified by the blood. Does this term boggle the mind? It need not. It is simple to grasp when the term *justification* is presented in laymen's language. Do the following. Break the word *justify* into syllables. The results: JUST-IF-I. Now add the words, HAD NEVER SINNED. There you have it in all of its magnificent simplicity: "JUST-IF-I-HAD NEVER SINNED." In other words, when one comes to Christ and has the shed blood applied for the remission of his personal sins, immediately, yea instantaneously, God looks upon that person as though he had never committed one single sin.

Is this possible? Yes, because God no longer sees the erring one, but He sees His Son and the merits of Christ's atoning blood covering the sinner. Say, isn't that startling news? You can have a new beginning in life today, for Jesus said, *Come unto me, all ye that labour and are heavy laden, and I will give you rest* (Matthew 11:28). Yes, all this is true for any and all who open their minds and hearts to Christ. When they do, they are *justified by his blood* (Romans 5:9). Yes, *...justified freely by his grace through the redemption that is in Christ Jesus...through faith in his blood...* (Romans 3:24,25). Why continue being a loser when blessing unspeakable simply awaits your decision?

We Experience Redemption Through the Blood

Third, one experiences redemption through Christ's blood. Is this terminology confusing? Does it sound like a name given to a center issuing gifts for S&H Green Stamps? Well, the gift about to be discussed dwarfs man's most esteemed prizes. Why? What is redemption? It is to deliver a thing or person by paying a price. It is to buy back something (see Leviticus 25:47-49).

Let me illustrate. God placed Adam and Eve under a test of obedience in the Garden of Eden. He said in Genesis 2:17, *But of the tree of the knowledge of good and evil, thou shalt not eat of it: for in the day that thou eatest thereof thou shalt surely die.* The slithering, slimy serpent said, *Ye shall not surely die* (Genesis 3:4). Eve listened to the devil rather than to God, for *...when the woman saw that the tree was good for food, and that it was pleasant to the eyes, and a tree to be desired to make one wise, she took of the fruit thereof, and did eat, and gave also unto her husband with her; and he did eat* (Genesis 3:6).

Immediately, this act of transgression brought sin into and upon the human race. This selling out of self to the devil placed all of Adam's descendants under Satan's bondage. That's why Romans 5:12 states, *Wherefore, as by one man* [Adam] *sin entered into the world, and death by sin; and so death passed upon all men, for that all have sinned.* Again, verse 18: *...by the offence of one* [Adam] *judgment came upon all men to condemnation....* Hence, because of Adam's transgression, we find ourselves in bondage to Satan—yes, sold out to the devil!

You ask, "Who will redeem us, buy us back, liberate us, and set us free?" None other than the Lord Jesus Christ our Saviour! It is He who paid the ransom price to buy us back from Satan's enslavement.

To fully appreciate what God will do for each of us, we must understand how another term, *ransom*, fits into this mighty work of redemption. In modern society, when a criminal kidnaps another person, he usually asks for ransom money to set the victim free. This is exactly what Christ did for sinners when He shed His blood. He paid the ransom price to buy back sinners. Matthew 20:28 states, *...the Son of man came...to give his life a ransom for many.* Also, *...there is...one mediator between God and men, the man Christ Jesus; Who gave himself a ransom for all...* (1 Timothy 2:5,6).

This means that you do not have to be a slave to debauchery. You do not have to be in bondage to sin for an entire lifetime. Christ wants to set you free. He longs that you experience *...redemption* *through his blood...* (Ephesians 1:7). WOW! It is joy unspeakable and full of glory to be redeemed through the *...precious blood of Christ...* (1 Peter 1:19).

Now let me illustrate what I have been saying with a thrilling story. Years ago, Dr. A. J. Gordon, after a long and tedious day, decided to take a walk for some relaxation. Soon he noticed a little boy from his Sunday school walking down the street with a cage full of sparrows.

He said, "Tommy, where are you going?"

"Preacher, I just caught these sparrows, and I am taking them home to my cat."

Dr. Gordon replied, "Tommy, that isn't very nice, is it? Let me tell you a better plan. I will buy the sparrows for a price."

"Oh, preacher, I could not sell you these birds because I would be cheating you. They are only insignificant sparrows."

But Dr. Gordon insisted, "Never mind, son, here is a dollar for each bird in your cage." The minister gave the little tyke $5, took the cage full of sparrows, prayed that none of his members would see him, dashed up an alley, opened the door of the cage, reached in, took out the sparrows, and hurled them into the air.

The next morning he related the episode in his sermon and said, "As the little birds flew into the heavenlies, I could almost hear them singing, 'Redeemed! How I love to proclaim it. Redeemed through Dr. Gordon's ransom money.'"

Friends, this is exactly what the Lord Jesus Christ did for lost humanity, for you and me. He shed His precious blood to pay the ransom price to set victimized sinners free. Receive this gift of love today and be redeemed! Let Christ buy you back from Adam's sell-out to Satan. When it happens, you will sing, "Redeemed! How I love to proclaim it. Redeemed by the blood of the Lamb."

Then, one day in eternity to come, in the presence of Christ himself, you will eternally sing redemption's story. Revelation 5:9 describes the momentous event. *And they sung a new song, saying, Thou are worthy* [Christ] *to take the book, and to open the seals thereof: for thou wast slain, and has redeemed us to God by thy blood out of every kindred, and tongue, and people, and nation.* What a song, and what a day it will be when the largest choir in history sings about the blood of Jesus Christ the Lamb. Those who refuse to sing about His shed blood now because of intellectual snobbery or rejection of the truth shall be unable to sing in heaven's greatest assembly. What a loss! Oh, get rid of all preconceived ideas and false reasonings today and trust in Christ's shed blood immediately for the remission of your sin!

Chapter 9

How Is Your Blood Pressure?

"There is a fountain filled with blood
    Drawn from Immanuel's veins,
And sinners plunged beneath that flood
    Lose all their guilty stains."

Christians lovingly sing this beautiful hymn which tells the gospel story in its totality. Christ came to earth to assume a body containing blood so that He might shed this liquid of life for you and me.

Today, Christendom freely talks about "the death of Christ for sinners," but death alone is insufficient if one is to be saved eternally. Christ could have died in numerous ways, but none of the methods of decease would have sufficed. For, you see, ...*it is the blood that maketh an atonement for the soul* (Leviticus 17:11), and ...*without shedding of blood* [there] *is no remission* [for sin] (Hebrews 9:22).

Is this merely my opinion or is it repeatedly taught in God's Holy Word? Listen carefully. The word *blood* occurs three times as often as the terminology *cross of Christ* and five times as frequently as *death of Christ*.

Christ's Cleansing Blood

In the previous chapter I mentioned that lost souls are saved, justified, and redeemed by the blood of Jesus. In this study we continue our discussion by triumphantly declaring that cleansing is also available to all through Christ's sacrifice. Now the question is, Is this shockingly important truth about the cleansing power of the blood of Christ in harmony with scientific truth? Get ready for some thrilling biological facts!

The great medical specialist Dr. Paul Brand encourages everyone to make the following experiment. Buy a blood pressure kit and wrap the cuff around the arm. When it is in position, have a friend pump it up to about 200mm of mercury, a sufficient pressure to stop the flow of blood in one's arm. Initially, the arm will feel an uncomfortable tightness beneath the cuff. Now comes the revealing part of the experiment. Perform an easy task with your cuffed arm. Merely flex your fingers and make a fist about ten times in succession or cut paper with scissors or drive a nail into wood with a hammer.

The first few movements will seem quite normal as the muscles obediently contract and relax. Soon, however, you will feel a slight weakness. Then, suddenly without warning, a hot flash of pain will strike after approximately ten movements. The muscles will cramp, and soon there will be a time of extreme agony. In fact, a continuance of movement will be impossible as the pain becomes unbearable. Next, as you release the pressure and air escapes from the cuff, blood will rush back into the aching arm and a wonderful sense of relief will be noticeable.

Now, why has all this happened? Physiologically, you have just experienced the cleansing power of the blood—your blood. While the blood supply to your arm was shut off, the continued forcing of the muscles to do the simplest chores converted the oxygen into energy, thereby producing waste products (called metabolites). These are normally flushed away instantly by the bloodstream. However, while the blood flow was hindered the poisons or toxins were accumulating in the cells causing horrendous pain. Then, as soon as the cuff was released, the swirling stream of blood "cleansed" and "washed away" all poisons, thus producing relief and joy. This is exactly what happens to one and all when the *...precious blood of Christ...* (1 Peter 1:19) is allowed to swirl away the poisons of sin accumulated over the years of separation from God.

May I ask you a question? "Have you been to Jesus for the cleansing power? Are you washed in the blood of the Lamb? There's a fountain flowing for the soul unclean; Oh, be washed in the blood of the Lamb." It does not matter how far one has gone in the paths of wickedness. The powerful, efficacious blood is potent enough—twenty centuries after being shed—to liquidate, obliterate, and exterminate all one's heinous past, for *...the blood of Jesus Christ his* [God's] *Son cleanseth us from all sin* (1 John 1:7).

First Corinthians 6:9-11 proves my assertion. *Know ye not that the unrighteous shall not inherit the kingdom of God? Be not deceived: neither for-*

*nicators, nor idolaters, nor adulterers, nor effemi-
nate, nor abusers of themselves with mankind,
Nor thieves, nor covetous, nor drunkards, nor
revilers, nor extortioners, shall inherit the kingdom of God. And such were some of you: but ye are
washed....* Amen, and amen! The vilest of sins are
mentioned in this horrendous listing, and yet
these sinners were washed.

Think of it! Fornicators (those who indulge in
premarital sex), idolaters, adulterers, homosexuals, thieves, drunkards, hate-filled gossipers, and
swindlers—all washed! Washed. Get it, WASHED!
Why? Because the blood of Christ is sufficient to
wash away man's worst degradations. We say,
Praise be *unto him that loved us, and washed us
from our sins in his own blood* (Revelation 1:5).

The truth is even more glorious since the
"cleansed" also have all their past forgiven and forgotten, because God says in Hebrews 8:12, *...their
sins and their iniquities will I remember no more.*
This is because the Father removes one's sins *as far
as the east is from the west...* (Psalm 103:12), and
casts all of our sins behind His back (see Isaiah
38:17). And if that isn't enough, He also casts all
our sins *...into the depths of the sea* (Micah 7:19),
and then puts up a sign that says, "NO FISHING
ALLOWED." Hallelujah!

This is why children in Sunday school so
vociferously sing:

"Gone, Gone, Gone, Gone! Yes, my sins are gone.

Now my soul is free, and in my heart's a song.

Buried in the deepest sea, Yes, that's good
enough for me.

I shall live eternally, Praise God! My sins are gone!"

Why don't you trust Jesus today and begin singing and making melody in your heart to the Lord (see Ephesians 5:19). You, too, may be part of the throng that ...*have washed their robes, and made them white in the blood of the Lamb* (Revelation 7:14).

We Have Been Sanctified

Now because of being saved, justified, redeemed, cleansed, and washed, we can assuredly know that we have been sanctified (or made holy) in God's sight because Christ [sanctified] *the people with his own blood...* (Hebrews 13:12). But wait! I have more good news! Eternal peace with God is also possible. No longer does one have to wonder about his state or standing with the Almighty. Jesus Christ is *The Prince of Peace* (Isaiah 9:6). This is not just a title, but a job description.

When Christ ascended Calvary's cross twenty centuries ago, something wonderful took place for every sinner—past, present, and future! Christ made eternal peace a possibility for all who trust in the merits of His shed blood. Now since He ...*made peace through the blood of his cross...* (Colossians 1:20), one may instantaneously experience this tranquility by receiving Jesus.

Are we finished? No, there is more glorious news as I tell you in conclusion that there is deliverance from the fear of death through Christ's precious blood. This comforting thought is discovered in

Hebrews 2:14,15. *As the children are partakers of flesh and blood* [their parents], *he also himself* [Christ] *likewise took part of the same* [flesh and blood]... as He came through the womb of the virgin Mary. At that time He bore a body which enabled Him to die like others, *...that through death he might destroy him that had the power of death, that is, the devil; And deliver them who through fear of death were all their lifetime subject to bondage.*

In simpler English, Christ came from heaven, took a body, died in that body, and destroyed the power Satan wielded over us concerning the fear of death. Thus, when one trusts in the shed blood of Christ, death's stinging bite is no longer feared. In fact, the trusting child of God can cry out with Paul, *...to die is gain* (Philippians 1:21) because *...to be absent from the body...* [is] *to be present with the Lord* (2 Corinthians 5:8). Why not enjoy this kind of comfort in a day of frustration. It is yours for the asking. Romans 10:13 states, *For whosoever shall call upon the name of the Lord shall be saved.*

Would you like to be saved eternally? Would it not be great to be cleansed from every sin—yes, all the hidden skeletons of past iniquities? Wouldn't it be a glorious feeling to know that every wicked blemish of your past and present lifestyle had been forgiven and forgotten because God had cast the whole abominable mess into the depths of the sea? Surely this thought alone would remove the fear of dying. Well, it can happen right now, this very moment, as one trusts in Jesus.

Chapter 10

The Last Seven Sayings of Christ Upon the Cross

Seven is the number of perfection and holiness, and Christ uttered seven cries from the tree that held His body in suspension between heaven and earth. Let's look at the seven sayings in order of their utterance and then analyze the tender compassionate heart of Christ. We will immediately notice that even the order or progress of the seven cries is Christlike, for He begins with His enemies and ends with himself. All through His life it was others first—self last. Thus Jesus died even as He had lived. The order is:

1. *Father, forgive them; for they know not what they do...* (Luke 23:34).
2. *To day shalt thou be with me in paradise* (Luke 23:43).
3. *Woman, behold thy son! ...Behold thy mother!* (John 19:26,27).
4. *My God, my God, why hast thou forsaken me?* (Matthew 27:46).
5. *I thirst* (John 19:28).
6. *It is finished* (John 19:30).
7. *Father, into thy hands I commend my spirit...* (Luke 23:46).

Oh, what love, what compassion, what heartache, and what suffering. It was all for us. Everyone at this point should repeat the latter part of Galatians 2:20, [Christ] *loved me, and gave himself for me.*

God's Love

Now, let's analyze each of these statements.

#1: The first thing Jesus did when He got to His cross was to seek forgiveness for those who had viciously nailed Him to it. He was beginning His ministry of intercession for His enemies by virtue of His blood—already freely flowing from His veins. This cry was not being made for His admirers and devotees, but for the rabble-rousers who had mercilessly mangled and mutilated His flesh. It was for the brutes who had used the Roman cat-o-nine-tails and shredded the skin of His chest, arms, and back. It was for the villains who had barbarously battered His face with sticks and fists and yanked His beard out by the roots (see Isaiah 50:6).

The sinners who had spit in His face ridiculing, vilifying, and disqualifying Him as the Saviour of the world were also part of His intercessory cry. Even the soldiers who had nailed His hands and feet to the tree and who dropped the cross into a hole with such vehemence and hatred that it dislocated His bones (see Psalm 22:14) were recipients of His tender supplications to His Father.

Oh, dear friend, God is love and He longs to save you regardless of the way you have treated Him. Christ died as He had lived. Do you remember His teachings contained in the Sermon on the Mount?

Matthew 5:44-48: *Love your enemies, bless them that curse you, do good to them that hate you, and pray for them which despitefully use you, and persecute you; That ye may be the children of your Father which is in heaven: for he maketh his sun to rise on the evil and on the good, and sendeth rain on the just and on the unjust. For if ye love them which love you, what reward have ye? do not even the publicans the same? And if ye salute your brethren only, what do ye more than others? do not even the publicans so? Be ye therefore perfect, even as your Father which is in heaven is perfect.*

Loving Our Enemies

Is it possible to manifest love toward those who hate us? After all, Christ was God in human flesh and thereby different from the rest of us. Oh, but He also was tested in all points as we are and was without sin (see Hebrews 4:15).

In order to prove that it is possible to love others who hate us, we turn our minds to the first Christian martyr, Stephen. In Acts 7, we find this spiritual giant preaching one of the strongest messages ever recorded. The ungodly worldlings couldn't take this bombardment of truth and reacted violently. Verse 54: *When they heard these things, they were cut to the heart, and they gnashed on him with their teeth.* This means that they gritted their teeth and hurled every profane, immoral oath imaginable into his face.

It didn't bother this saint in the least for *...he, being full of the Holy Ghost, looked up stedfastly into heaven, and saw the glory of God, and Jesus standing on the right hand of God, And said, Behold, I see the heavens opened, and the Son of man standing on the right hand of God* (verses

55,56). This raised the anger of the crowd to an unusual pitch for, *Then they cried out with a loud voice, and stopped their ears, and ran upon him with one accord, And cast him out of the city, and stoned him...* (verses 57,58).

Now get the picture—don't miss it—because here we find the real evidence of the Holy Spirit in a human's life. Notice it is not in words but in actions. The great sign is not speaking in supernatural languages but love for one's enemies, who in Stephen's case, crushed his skull with rocks. Notice verse 55: *...he, being full of the Holy Ghost....* The result: *And he kneeled down, and cried with a loud voice, Lord, lay not this sin to their charge. And when he had said this, he fell asleep* [or he died] (verse 60). This is the evidence of the Holy Spirit's operation in a life that a sin-riddled, hateful world wants to observe.

#2: The second expression, *To day shalt thou be with me in paradise*, is closely aligned with the first in that the Saviour forgives one individual who has shown nothing but hatred toward Him. In the Gospel accounts we find both thieves heckling Christ. Mark 15:32: *...they* [plural] *that were crucified with him reviled him.*

The religious leaders said, *He saved others; himself he cannot save. If he be the King of Israel, let him now come down from the cross, and we will believe him. He trusted in God; let him deliver him now, if he will have him: for he said, I am the Son of God* (Matthew 27:42,43). Now look at verse 44: *The thieves also, which were crucified with him, cast the same in his teeth* [or face].

Since both thieves were making these identical statements and accusations against Christ's saving ability, what triggered the sudden change of attitude in the one convict? I believe it was love. This thief saw the hatred the world had heaped upon Christ as well as upon himself. His heart was so incensed with the brutes who nailed him to a tree next to Christ that he would have strangled his executioners with his bare hands had it been possible.

Then, as he looked at the center cross and saw Christ, he heard an unbelievable utterance falling from the Lord's lips: *Father, forgive them; for they know not what they do* (Luke 23:34). The thief was startled by the love shown to such villains. It was superhuman. Because of it, he suddenly changed his mind about Christ. Soon the one who hurled infamous blasphemies at Christ called upon Him for salvation. His cry was, *Lord, remember me when thou comest into thy kingdom* (Luke 23:42).

Did Christ really forgive this one who so hatefully slandered Him? Did Jesus mean what He prayed when He said, "Father, forgive them"? The answer is tenderly given in the second expression: *To day shalt thou be with me in paradise* (verse 43).

Dear friend, Christ will also forgive you of any sin if you will open your mind and heart to Him. Your sin may be murder, abortion, alcoholism, drug addiction, adultery, fornication, homosexuality, blasphemy, thievery, lying, or some other enslaving vice. Hear it! First John 1:7: *...the blood of Jesus Christ his Son cleanseth us from all sin.* The thief was out of Christ in the morning, in Christ at noon, and with Christ in the evening. Guilt, grace, and glory are the three stages in the spiritual biography of the thief on the cross.

#3: The third statement ringing from the Saviour's lips also resounds the message of love. Let's turn from the outer circle of sin-blinded religious leaders, brutal soldiers, and hardened criminals to the inner circle of believers. The lesson unfolded now is very moving.

Mary was the instrument of God used to bring His Son into the world. This pure young lady was a virgin who had never known man in an intimate way (see Luke 1:34). She became impregnated through the miracle-working power of the Holy Spirit—a special act of creation (see Luke 1:35). Therefore Joseph had nothing to do with the birth of Christ and was only called his father because he adopted Christ. As Christ hung upon the cruel cross, dying for the sins of an entire world, Joseph was not present—all evidence suggests that he was already dead.

Jesus looked at the lonely little woman who bore Him and His tender heart was grieved. He wanted assurance that someone would take care of Mother after His departure. He looked at Mary and at His beloved disciple John and said, *Woman, behold thy son! ...Behold thy mother!* (John 19:26,27). Yes, Christ in His dying moments was concerned about the future welfare of Mary who had borne Him and whose soul was now pierced with a sword (see Luke 2:35).

Jesus had no earthly possessions to leave His mother (see 2 Corinthians 8:9). He brought nothing into the world at His birth, and He had nothing to leave behind as He left this life. He died as poor as He had lived. All that He could leave His mother was His love. He wanted His followers to love as He loved. Jesus said in Matthew 19:19, *Honour thy father and thy mother....*

What a lesson there is for this thoughtless, cruel age in which we live. Thousands weep because they have been forgotten. Lord, forgive us for we know not what we do. Love is the proof of salvation—love for parents, for in-laws, for believers, for neighbors, and for lowly sinners. Do you have the evidence?

First John 4:7,8 says, *Beloved, let us love one another: for love is of God; and every one that loveth is born of God, and knoweth God. He that loveth not knoweth not God; for God is love.* John 13:35: *By this shall all men know that ye are my disciples, if ye have love one to another.* If this element of love pictured in the first three sayings of the cross is missing in your life, find out why. Are you saved? Are you filled with the Holy Spirit? Seek that love which proves salvation is real.

In closing our examination of these statements revealing God's love, let me ask you a personal question. Would you be ready to meet Christ today if you were to die? Christ said to the repentant thief, *To day shalt thou be with me in paradise* (Luke 23:43). It is blessed to have the assurance that one will be with Christ for all eternity. He died by the shedding of blood, was buried, and rose again for your sins. Have you accepted this truth and received Him?

God's Holiness

#4: The fourth cry, *My God, my God, why hast thou forsaken me?* (Matthew 27:46) reveals the holiness of God and the depravity of man. *God is love* (1 John 4:8). However, this does not mean that He sentimentally allows man's ungodliness and debased practices to go unpunished. Perish the thought! He is also a God of holiness and wants mankind to partake of this righteous attribute. First Peter 1:16 says, *Be ye holy; for I am holy.*

The problem is that man is inherently wicked. Every member of the human race arrives on the scene with the nature of Adam. Romans 5:12: *Wherefore, as by one man sin entered into the world, and death by sin; and so death passed upon all men, for that all have sinned.* Yes, every one of us is born with this sinful, wicked, Adamic nature. It is this sin principle with which we are born that makes us lie, cheat, swindle, curse, blaspheme, and become enslaved to every known vice that mankind creates. We do not become sinners because we commit these abominable practices, but rather we practice these wicked iniquities because we were born with a nature that hungers after sin.

Because the God of holiness cannot look upon sin, and because this God of holiness is also a God of love, we begin to understand the words of the Saviour, *My God, my God, why hast thou forsaken me?* At the cross, God's two attributes of holiness and love were made manifest—His love, in that His Son was being offered to rid mankind of sin; His holiness, as He forsook the Son He loved. Romans 8:32 says that God *spared not His own Son.*

The reason the Father turned His back upon His Son, refusing to look at Him was that, at Calvary, Christ was covered from head to toe with every loathsome sin mankind had ever and would ever commit. Please remember that Christ was not dying for His own sin. He was the Holy One of God *who did no sin* (1 Peter 2:22). *He...knew no sin* (2 Corinthians 5:21). He was *holy, harmless, undefiled, separate from sinners* (Hebrews 7:26). The "good news" is *that Christ died for **our** sins* (1 Corinthians 15:3). He *loved us, and washed us from our sins in His own blood* (Revelation 1:5).

As Jesus hung there stained, saturated, and sin-laden, the Father refused to look at His Son. Why? Christ was bearing every vile, degrading vice that depraved human beings had ever committed or would ever commit. His body and soul were completely immersed with man's abominations. He bore the disobedience of Adam, the murderous act of Cain, the adultery of David, and the murders of the Christians by Saul of Tarsus. He bore every sin committed since the inception of history and every sin which will be committed until the world disintegrates by fire.

Christ bore adultery, anger, blasphemy, burglary, carnality, corruption, covetousness, cursing, deceit, defilement, degeneracy, dishonour, drunkenness, drug addiction, envy, extortion, filthiness, fornication, guile, hatred, harlotry, homosexuality, heresy, hypocrisy, jealousy, lasciviousness, lying, murder, nudity, perversion, profanity, rebellion, revenge, robbery, sadism, seduction, stealing, swearing, thievery, unfaithfulness, ungodliness, vileness, violence, war, whoredom, whoremongering, wickedness, and every sin that may have escaped this lengthy listing.

Never in the annals of history had so much sin been carried at one time, and it was all carried by the sinless One. It was all upon the sinless, holy, God-man, Christ Jesus, and this is why the Father turned away from the voice of His Son as Christ took our place (see Psalm 22:1). God could not look upon the scene. Truly, it was our sin, our wickedness, our transgressions, our iniquities, and our abominations that turned God's face from the heartbreaking event.

#5: Christ had suffered severe abuse at the hands of His tormentors. Many were His anguished cries. Psalm 22:1 tells us that He literally roared upon that cruel tree because of the excruciating pain. Naturally, His mouth became parched, pasty, and dry. Thus He cried, *I thirst* (John 19:28).

What a paradox that Christ, the Water of life, the One who satisfies the eternal thirst of the soul, cried for water. The blessing of these words becomes understandable when one realizes that the God-man was willing to suffer physical thirst in order that our spiritual thirst might be quenched for all eternity.

This truth is taught in John 4:13,14. Jesus, conversing with the woman at the well, said, *Whosoever drinketh of this water shall thirst again.* Why? Mankind must continually replenish the fluid in his body or death will ensue. *But,* Christ continued, *...whosoever drinketh of the water that I shall give him shall never thirst; but the water that I shall give him shall be in him a well of water springing up into everlasting life.*

I personally drank of this water many years ago, and the Lord has satisfied every desire and longing in my heart. Quit trying to quench the thirst of your spiritual being with liquor, drugs, sex, pleasure, or money. Drink of the water of life freely. God's invitation to you is found in the last chapter of the Bible, Revelation 22:17: *...let him that is athirst come. And whosoever will, let him take the water of life freely.* It is yours without money, without works, without man-made rites and ceremonies, without Lenten observations. God offers it freely. *The gift of God is eternal life through Jesus Christ our Lord* (Romans 6:23).

Christ Finished the Plan

#6: The sixth utterance is the greatest statement ever recorded, historically. *It is finished* (John 19:30). The original Greek does not carry three words, but one: *finished.*

Friend, do you get the significance of this statement? Does it simply mean that Christ expired or died upon a tree as far as your understanding of the subject is concerned? If so, get ready for some thrilling theological truth. The terminology *It is finished* had to do with the eternal plan the Trinity originated in heaven before the world was created.

As we learned in chapter 3, the Father, Son, and Holy Spirit sat down in the counsels of eternity past and meticulously planned redemption's program. They decided that the sacrifice of shed blood would be the only means of salvation for mankind. Blood would make atonement for the soul (see Leviticus 17:11). At first, animal blood would be a temporary offering—only covering sin until a permanent sacrifice could be made. Since mankind's blood was tainted through the fall of its father, Adam, there could only be one solution. A member of the Godhead would have to go to earth, take a body with blood, and shed that blood to take away the sin that animal blood could only cover.

First Peter 1:20 proves this teaching. *Who* [Christ] *verily was foreordained before the foundation of the world....* Revelation 13:8 states that Christ is *...the Lamb slain from the foundation of the world.* When was He slain? Before and from the foundation of the world.

Christ said in Hebrews 10:4,5, *For it is not possible that the blood of bulls and of goats should take away sins. Wherefore...a body hast thou prepared me.* This prepared body had blood. It was pure, holy blood because of the virgin birth. It was not contaminated with Adam's virus of sin. John the Baptist recognized Christ's earthly mission and victoriously cried out in John 1:29, *Behold the Lamb of God, which taketh away the sin of the world.* Animal blood had covered sin to this point, but soon Christ, God's Lamb, would shed His blood and take away the sin that was hitherto covered.

When Christ shed His blood at Calvary, He cried, *Finished!* The programmed plan from eternity past had now come to completion. The shedding of blood was finished forever. Hebrews 9:12 says, *Neither by the blood of goats and calves, but by his own blood he entered in once into the holy place, having obtained eternal redemption for us.* Hebrews 10:12 states that *...he...offered one sacrifice for sins for ever....* This is why it is finished. He did it once for all—and forever. This is why man's works are useless. It is the work of Christ—and only the work of Christ—that is sufficient forever.

#7: *...into thy hands I commend my spirit* (Luke 23:46). In essence, Christ was saying, "Father, You sent Me into the world (see Galatians 4:4). My work upon Calvary's cross is finished. I have shed My blood for the sins of the world. Now I commend My Spirit unto You."

What a beautiful example Christ sets in this last utterance from the cross. He is at perfect peace and is soon going home. The liberals and apostacized religionists of our day may laugh about heaven. They may try to insult real Christians with such phraseology as "pie in the sky when you die by and by." Yet, death must and will come for every member of Adam's race and there is nothing more satisfying than the assurance of eternal life. What joy and satisfaction there is when one believes the Word of God and the sayings of Jesus—especially when the night of death approaches.

Does it bother you to think about the inevitability of decease? It does not have to be this way. Death is not a sad ending but a glorious beginning for those who have trusted in Christ. He who said, *Into thy hands I commend my spirit,* also said in John 14:1-3, *Let not your heart be troubled: ye believe in God, believe also in me. In my Father's house are many mansions: if it were not so, I would have told you. I go to prepare a place for you. And if I go and prepare a place for you, I will come again, and receive you unto myself; that where I am, there ye may be also.* Verse 6: *I am the way, the truth, and the life: no man cometh unto the Father, but by me.* He died, was buried, and rose again for us. That's the gospel. Where He went, you can go—if He lives in your heart. Receive Him now!

Chapter 11

The Importance of
Christ's Resurrection

On June 18, 1815, twelve miles south of Brussels and two miles from the Belgian village of Waterloo—largely through a series of mistakes and misunderstandings among his own leaders—Napoleon was soundly defeated by Arthur Wellesley, better known as the Duke of Wellington. At the time of this victory, one of the strangest events in the annals of England's history took place.

Without our modern means of communication, the people in those days were limited to semaphore signals. The news of Wellington's decisive victory was passed along until finally, in the last relay from a ship out in the channel, the message was passed on to receivers stationed high in the towers of Westminster Abbey. The communication stated, "Wellington defeated."

When those two words were received, a heavy fog rolled across London and the message—just as received—was passed on to the waiting people. All of London was filled with grief and despair as strong men sobbed openly and women agonized in the streets. However, a few hours later another wind blew the fog away, and the message from the ship began again, this time adding a third word and reading, "Wellington defeated Napoleon."

What a difference! The first message said, "Wellington defeated," and the fog stopped the third word. But later the message said, "Wellington defeated Napoleon." Oh, the rejoicing that took place in England when they got the third word of that message.

A similar event took place at Calvary. On the day of the crucifixion, the fog of hell seemed to roll in with its message, "Christ defeated." That day ended with a broken, bloody, dead Messiah and scattered, weeping, defeated disciples. Then, three days and three nights later the fog was dispelled by the brightness of glory. Special archangels from heaven descended to earth and rolled back the stone from the empty tomb so that a waiting world could read the entire message, "Christ defeated Satan." Hallelujah! Christ defeated Satan. Praise God for the resurrection of Jesus Christ.

You Must Believe in the Resurrection

We are living in a day and age when many apostate, liberal, modernistic ministers scoff at the resurrection. Dr. Duncan E. Littlefair has a book entitled *The Changing Religious Thought.* I quote from pages 104 and 105. Listen to this blasphemy: "The resurrection is not peculiar to Christianity. Don't you go building religion on this basis. Don't build it on the idea that somehow or another something different happened in Christianity because Jesus was raised from the dead. It is not so. It just isn't so. I say to you that this physical resurrection must stop being a dominant thing in our minds. We have to understand it differently. We must see it with our spiritual eyes. The virgin birth is a mytho-logical tale."

This is a minister speaking! Well, I choose to believe God (see Acts 27:25)! Matthew 1:23 says, *Behold, a virgin shall be with child....* Let's listen to God rather than men.

Dr. Littlefair continues, "The virgin birth is a story designed to say something. It wasn't meant to be understood physically. It was a picturesque way of telling something wonderful that couldn't be told any other way. The resurrection story is the same." It should not be taken *physically?*

Wait a minute! Let's see what God has to say. In Luke 24:39, Jesus appeared to His disciples after the crucifixion and the resurrection, and He was in a body. He said, *Behold my hands and my feet, that it is I myself* [you do not believe it?]: *handle me, and see* [come on and touch me!]; *for a spirit hath not flesh and bones, as ye see me have.* Dr. Littlefair says that it should not be taken literally, as far as the physical is concerned!

He further states, "Don't take it with your crude literal hands and destroy it. A rolled away stone and some clothes left there—how trivial and insignificant." Really? The literal, physical resurrection is insignificant? Oh, Dr. Littlefair, how about Romans 10:9,10 which says that if you do not believe in this literal resurrection you cannot be saved? *That if thou shalt confess with thy mouth the Lord Jesus, and shalt believe in thine heart that God hath raised him from the dead, thou shalt be saved. For with the heart man believeth unto righteousness; and with the mouth confession is made unto salvation.*

Dr. Littlefair goes on to say, "Two men sitting there announced that the body was no longer there. One of the disciples putting his finger into the wound in the side, Jesus eating a fish to show that He was physical, passing through a wall to give a miracle, and, finally, rising up with His body. If you stop to think about it you realize the absurdity of it."

Sir, the only absurdity I see is in the article you have written in your book which does away with the precious story of what the Holy Bible, God's Word, has to say about the resurrection.

In one paragraph, this accomplished apostate denies the virgin birth, the resurrection, the ascension, the existence of heaven, and the integrity of the Holy Scriptures. Philippians 3:10 says, *That I may know him, and the power of his resurrection....* Let me tell you, when you really know Jesus—not about Jesus, but know Him with your heart—you also know the power of the resurrection. You know it is not just myth. You know that it is real.

In 2 Peter 1:16, the apostle says, *For we have not followed cunningly devised fables, when we made known unto you the power and coming of our Lord Jesus Christ, but were eyewitnesses of his majesty.* In other words, Peter says, "This is not something that we hatched up in a dream—it is something that we saw with our own eyes."

The pages of the Holy Bible are literally saturated with resurrection truth. Job 19:25: *For I know that*

The Importance of Christ's Resurrection

*my redeemer liveth, and that he shall stand at the
latter day upon the earth.*

In Mark 16:6 the angel says, *Be not affrighted: Ye
seek Jesus of Nazareth, which was crucified: he is
risen....*

In John 11:25 Jesus Christ says, *I am the resurrection, and the life....*

Peter, preaching in Acts 5:30, says, *The God of
our fathers raised up Jesus....*

Romans 4:25: *Who was delivered for our
offences, and was raised again for our
justification.*

Romans 8:34: *Who is he that condemneth? It is
Christ that died, yea rather, that is risen again,
who is even at the right hand of God....*

First Corinthians 15:3,4: *Christ died for our
sins... And...he was buried, and...he rose again
the third day according to the scriptures.*

First Thessalonians 1:10: *And to wait for his Son
from heaven, whom he raised from the dead....*

Second Timothy 2:8: *Remember that Jesus
Christ of the seed of David was raised from the
dead....*

Hebrews 13:20,21: *Now the God of peace, that
brought again from the dead our Lord Jesus, that
great shepherd of the sheep...Make you perfect....*

Revelation 1:18: *I am he that liveth, and was
dead; and, behold, I am alive for evermore....*
There is one thing this Book teaches and that is the
story of the resurrection.

Our Faith Depends on the Resurrection

I want to show you how vain, how empty, how
meaningless, and how futile the Christian religion

would be without the resurrection. I believe the greatest chapter on the subject is 1 Corinthians 15. Look at verses 1-8: *Moreover, brethren, I declare unto you the gospel which I preached unto you, which also ye have received, and wherein ye stand; By which also ye are saved....* What is that gospel? Verses 3-4: *...how that Christ died for our sins according to the scriptures; And that he was buried, and that he rose again the third day....*

Then God, through Paul, goes to the trouble of giving us the witnesses who saw Christ in His new body, for He says in verses 5-8: *...he was seen of Cephas, then of the twelve: After that, he was seen of above*[or over]*five hundred brethren at once.... After that, he was seen of James; then of all the apostles. And last of all he was seen of me also....*

Does it really matter whether or not one accepts the resurrection story? I have already quoted Romans 10:9, *That if thou shalt confess with thy mouth the Lord Jesus, and shalt believe in thine heart that God hath raised him from the dead, thou shalt be saved.*

You cannot be saved unless you believe the resurrection story. Why? Read 1 Corinthians 15:12-19: *Now if Christ be preached that he rose from the dead, how say some among you that there is no resurrection of the dead? But if there be no resurrection of the dead, then is Christ not risen: And if Christ be not risen, then is our preaching vain, and your faith is also vain. Yea, and we are found false witnesses of God; because we have testified of God that he raised up Christ: whom he raised not up, if so be that the dead rise not. For if the dead rise not, then is not Christ raised: And if Christ be not raised, your faith is vain; ye are yet in your sins. Then they also which are fallen asleep in Christ are perished. If in this life only we have hope in Christ, we are of all men most miserable.* Now here is the victorious note—*But now is Christ risen from the dead, and become the first-fruits of them that slept* (verse 20).

There are a number of points here that we need to see. First of all, if Christ be not risen, then our preaching is vain (verse 14). *Vain* means "empty" or "meaningless." Why? We would be preaching about a deceiver.

Jesus made some startling predictions. He said in Matthew 12:39,40, *An evil and adulterous generation seeketh after a sign; and there shall no sign be given to it, but the sign of the prophet Jonas: For as Jonas was three days and three nights in the whale's belly; so shall the Son of man be three days and three nights in the heart of the earth.* Hear Jesus again in Matthew 16:21, *From that time forth began Jesus to shew unto his disciples, how that he must go unto Jerusalem, and suffer many things of the elders and chief priests and scribes, and be killed, and be raised again the third day.*

Jesus said in John 2:19, *Destroy this temple* [this body], *and in three days I will raise it up.* He said, in effect, "They are going to kill Me; I will be in a grave for three days, but I am coming out of that grave." If He had not done that, all our preaching would be in vain because we would be preaching about a deceiver who predicted many things and never fulfilled them.

We would also be preaching about one who had taught erroneously. If He could not back up the teaching of the resurrection, then He would not be able to back up the teaching of the new birth when He said in John 3:7, *Ye must be born again.* He would not be able to back up the teaching of heaven when He said in John 14:2, *In my Father's house are many mansions....* He would not be able to back up the teaching of salvation when He said in John 14:6, *I am the way, the truth, and the life: no man cometh unto the Father, but by me.* But, praise God, He is risen and He is not a deceiver. We can believe every one of His teachings.

Second, our faith is also vain (verse 14). Why? Because one is trusting in a Saviour who could not produce what He had promised. He said, "I will come out of the grave the third day." If He did not do it, He would not have kept His promises. If He could not keep that promise, He could not keep the others He made.

For instance, John 8:12: *I am the light of the world: he that followeth me shall not walk in darkness, but shall have the light of life.*

John 10:9: *I am the door: by me if any man enter in, he shall be saved....*

John 11:25,26: *I am the resurrection, and the life: he that believeth in me, though he were dead, yet shall he live: And whosoever liveth and believeth in me shall never die....*

John 14:6: *I am the way, the truth, and the life: no man cometh unto the Father, but by me.*

The Importance of Christ's Resurrection

If He could not fulfill the promise of His resurrection, He would not be able to fulfill these other promises. Therefore, our faith would be in vain because we would be trusting in one who could not fulfill what He had promised. Praise God, Christ is risen and we can accept every promise. Because He fulfilled the first promise concerning His resurrection, He will fulfill all the rest. He will be the Light of the world to you. He will be the Door to heaven. He will be the Way. He will be your Resurrection and Life if you will let Him into your heart today.

Third, we are found false witnesses (verse 15). Why? *Because we have testified of God that he raised up Christ: whom he raised not up, if so be that the dead rise not.* Matthew would have lied because he recorded the resurrection story in chapter 28. He said in verse 6, *...he is risen....* Mark would have lied, for he recorded the same story in chapter 16. He triumphantly cried out in verse 6, *...he is risen; he is not here: behold the place where they laid him.*

Luke also would have been a prevaricator because he described the blessed resurrection in a narrative found in Luke 24. He said in verse 3, *And they entered in, and found not the body of the Lord Jesus.* Why? Because He was risen. John would have been untruthful because he unfolded the resurrection scene in John 20. The Apostle Peter would have been a false witness because he said in Acts 3:15, [You] *killed the Prince of life, whom God hath raised from the dead....*

All of these men would have been false witnesses or liars had they preached these truths, knowing that Christ's body had been stolen. However, they were filled with the blessed Holy Spirit and integrity. The greatest proof that they believed the message they declared is the fact that they went through horrible torture and death for the message they proclaimed.

Do you think a man would give his life if he did not really believe what he was preaching? Matthew's body was run through with a spear. Mark was dragged through the streets of Alexandria until the skin was torn off his body and his blood seeped into the sand. Then he died. Luke was hanged, and John was thrown into boiling oil. Peter was crucified, and Paul was beheaded.

These men would not have given their lives if they knew it had been a concocted message. No, praise God, let's say it again, He is risen! That is why these men were not false witnesses and why they even gave their lives for the message they preached.

Fourth, if there be no resurrection, *Then they also which are fallen asleep in Christ* [for those who have died in Christ] *are perished* (verse 18). If Christ perished, then we which are in Christ shall perish. If Christ had not been able to overcome death, then we who are in Christ shall certainly not be able to overcome death, because our energy, strength, and life must come from Him.

Our Saviour said in John 14:19, *...because I live, ye shall live also.* Let me tell you this: Because He is risen (praise God), all of our loved ones who died in Jesus are now in the presence of the Lord. Because He has eternal life in Him, He can give us this eternal life. Christ spoke the truth when He said in John 11:25 and 26, *I am the resurrection, and the life: he that believeth in me, though he were dead, yet shall he live: And whosoever liveth and believeth in me shall never die.* You can have life—eternal life—if you will come to this Jesus.

Finally, if Christ be not risen, *...we are of all men most miserable* (verse 19). Of course! Why? Because our preaching would be vain. Our faith would be vain. We would be false witnesses, and we would perish. Let me say it one more time. HE IS RISEN! Our preaching is not vain, and our faith is not vain. We are not found false witnesses, and we shall never perish. We shall be with Jesus for the ages of ages. Oh, let Him into your heart today!

Chapter 12

Ten Suggestions or Commandments?

Multitudes are convinced that they possess salvation. However, the reasons they give for being saved are erroneous. They talk about their efforts to please God and gain heaven. They mention baptism, confirmation, the Golden Rule, the Sermon on the Mount, and the Ten Commandments as means of salvation. How sad! While it is true that God gave us many of these wonderful ordinances, rules, and commands, it is equally true that none of them were ever presented to mankind as a means of obtaining eternal life. God gave us something greater—He gave us His own Son.

John 3:16, the gospel in a nutshell, states, *For God so loved the world, that he gave His only begotten Son, that whosoever believeth in him should not perish,but have everlasting life.* This Christ is the only way. All of man's meritorious efforts fall flat, because salvation is through the blood of the Lord Jesus Christ. Therefore, *He that hath the Son hath life; and he that hath not the Son of God hath not life* (1 John 5:12). In the light of this introduction, let us investigate God's purpose in presenting to the world His glorious Ten Commandments.

The Law's Purpose

Contrary to most modern thinking, the Commandments were never given to save men's souls.

For the law made nothing perfect... (Hebrews 7:19). Therefore, one must find another reason for Sinai's demands. It is found in Romans 3:20 which declares, *...by the law is the knowledge of sin....*

Again, James tells us in chapters 1 and 2 that God's law is like a mirror. It reflects one's image, reveals the dirt, and drives the soiled sinner to Christ for cleansing. The mirror cannot change the condition, only reveal the situation. It is Christ who *...loved us, and washed us from our sins in his own blood* (Revelation 1:5).

This is the clear meaning of Galatians 2:21 which states, *...if righteousness come by the law* [Ten Commandments], *then Christ is dead in vain.* How useless Christ's death is if man can produce his own salvation by following a code of ethics or a series of commands. Because this is an impossibility, God sent His Son to shed His sinless blood for hopeless transgressors. By doing this, He said once, for all, and forever, *This is the way, walk ye in it...* (Isaiah 30:21).

So, we see that the Law was never intended to save, but rather to reflect one's sinful condition and then to condemn and to destroy the sinner. That is why Romans 4:15 states, *...the law worketh wrath...* and 2 Corinthians 3:6 declares, *...the letter killeth....* This is its purpose—not salvation. *...for by the works of the law* [Ten Commandments] *shall no flesh be justified* (Galatians 2:16). With this explanatory background, let us look in the mirror and see if we have sinful faces.

The Ten Commandments

God's Ten Commandments are found in Exodus 20:3-17. They are as follows:

Thou shalt have no other gods before me.

Thou shalt not make unto thee any graven image, or any likeness of any thing that is in heaven above, or that is in the earth beneath, or that is in the water under the earth.

Thou shalt not take the name of the Lord thy God in vain....

Remember the sabbath day, to keep it holy.

Honour thy father and thy mother....

Thou shalt not kill.

Thou shalt not commit adultery.

Thou shalt not steal.

Thou shalt not bear false witness against thy neighbour.

Thou shalt not covet [desire] *thy neighbour's house...wife, nor...any thing that is thy neighbour's.*

Millions simply cry, "I have never broken any of the laws of God." Even the rich young ruler audaciously uttered such nonsense. What folly! A simple probe into the New Testament's interpretations of the Commandments silences the arrogant forever.

God gave His laws *...that every mouth may be stopped, and all the world may become guilty before God* (Romans 3:19). Yes, He gave these standards to shut the mouths of self-righteous humans who constantly boast about their morality, works, and goodness. Friend, *There is none righteous...* (Romans 3:10). Let's prove this statement as each commandment speaks for itself. Hear God!

The Commandments Interpreted

1. *Thou shalt have no other gods before me.* One may think that because he is not a Buddhist, Mohammedan, or a Moonite he automatically is absolved from all guilt concerning this first commandment, but Satan is the *...god of this world...* (2 Corinthians 4:4). When one places material values before spiritual blessings, he automatically bows at the wrong shrine. He worships another god. That god may be one's home, car, family, or money.

   Jesus said in Matthew 6:24, *No man can serve two masters* [two gods]: *for either he will hate the one, and love the other; or else he will hold to the one, and despise the other. Ye cannot serve God and mammon.* Imagine, Christ called money another god, and millions worship filthy lucre today. That is why they cheat, lie, and even rob God of His tithes (see Malachi 3:8).

2. *Thou shalt not make unto thee any graven image, or any likeness of any thing that is in heaven above, or that is in the earth beneath, or that is in the water under the earth. Thou shalt not bow down thyself to them....* God hates idolatry. Three times in Romans 1, we find the words, *God gave*

them up. God was appalled at the abominable practices of the people and gave them over to their vile desires.

One of the sins that grieved Jehovah God was they *...changed the glory of the uncorruptible God into an image made like to corruptible man...* (Romans 1:23). Idolatry is so loathed by God that Revelation 21:8 says, *...idolaters, and all liars, shall have their part in the lake which burneth with fire and brimstone: which is the second death.* Is it any wonder that God cries, *Little children, keep yourselves from idols* (1 John 5:21).

3. *Thou shalt not take the name of the Lord thy God in vain; for the Lord will not hold him guiltless that taketh his name in vain.* This commandment is broken millions of times daily. *God* is used to damn everyone and everything in this age of blasphemy. Ladies have become hardened in their usage of gutter language. Scores, even among the socially elite, sound like tramps. Romans 3:14,18 truly pictures today's society. *Whose mouth is full of cursing and bitterness,* and *There is no fear of God before their eyes.*

Rexella and I were seated near a group of cursing women in a restaurant. Their language was fit only for a brothel. When I heard one of them curse my God, I walked to their table and said, "I wonder if you women would watch your language, because I have a lady at the next table!" These liberated sinners could have gnashed me to death with their false teeth after that shocking episode! Wow!

If this bothered them, think of their fate when they meet God at the Judgment Day, for ...*the Lord will not hold him* [or her] *guiltless that taketh his name in vain.*

At this point may I caution many of you who use euphemisms that are equally blasphemous. A number of dictionaries mention the following terms as profane shortcuts in cursing God: *Gee, Gee-whiz, Gees, Oh, my God, Gosh, Golly,* and a slew of others. The Bible states, ...*holy and reverend is his name* (Psalm 111:9). Let's praise His matchless name!

4. Which day is the Sabbath? Is it Saturday? On which day should a Christian worship? I believe it is Sunday. The Saturday Sabbath was given to Israel. Ezekiel 20:12,20 states: *I gave them* [Israel] *my sabbaths, to be a sign between me and them, that they might know that I am the Lord...* and also ...*hallow my sabbaths; and they shall be a sign between me and you* [Israel].... This was the first covenant to Israel.

Christians have a new covenant, *Jesus made a surety of a better testament* (Hebrews 7:22). *He* [Christ] *is the mediator of a better covenant...* (Hebrews 8:6). *He* [Christ] *is the mediator of the new testament* [or new agreement] (Hebrews 9:15).

Because of His death and this new agreement, we are no longer under ceremonial laws involving days. Moral laws are in effect in believer's hearts, but not the ceremonial laws. Proof? God says in Colossians 2:14,16 that Christ [blotted] *out the handwriting of ordinances that was against us, which was contrary to us, and took it out of the way, nailing it to his cross.... Let no man therefore judge you in meat, or in drink, or in respect of an holyday, or of the new moon, or* [Get it!] *of the sabbath days.*

We are ...*not under law, but under grace* (Romans 6:14). God's moral law is written within and upon the hearts of believers, but ceremonial laws involving days have been nailed to the cross. We honor the Saviour of the new covenant on a new day—the day of His resurrection, which is Sunday, the first day of the week. This we do out of love, not servitude, not through law, but through grace.

5. *Honour thy father and thy mother....* This commandment is being flung to the winds by many young people who claim to love God. However, if one really loves God, he will love the words of God. Jehovah says, *Honour your parents.* Christ repeats the command in Matthew 19:19, and Paul says in Ephesians 6:1-3, *Children obey your parents in the Lord: for this is right. Honour thy father and mother; (which is the first commandment with promise;) That it may be well with thee, and thou mayest live long on the earth.* Did you notice that God pronounces a special blessing upon those who love and

honour their parents, the blessing of a long life? It is so important that neglect along these lines should be confessed immediately.

6. *Thou shalt not kill.* I will not waste time expounding this particular commandment. In fact, thousands of "murderers" may be reading this study this very moment. Why are you murderers? Because you hate your mother-in-law or your daughter-in-law. You would like to throw your son-in-law out the window—head first! Some are ready to smash the face of a neighbor and let him have it the second time as he turns his cheek.

Some hate the preacher and his family. Others malign the deacons or church members or anyone who disagrees with them one iota. Guess what? That's murder, for, *Whosoever hateth his brother is a murderer: and ye know that no murderer hath eternal life abiding in him* (1 John 3:15). Be sure you are saved for, *He that loveth not knoweth not God...* (1 John 4:8).

7. *Thou shalt not commit adultery.* Are you blameless along this line? You say, "Yes, sir. I have always been faithful to the little lady." Wait a minute. Jesus said, *...whosoever looketh on a woman to lust after her hath committed adultery with her already in his heart* (Matthew 5:28).

You say, "Not guilty! I have never had an impure thought in my life." I will get you when we hit the ninth commandment, Thou shalt not lie! But first, let's look at number eight.

8. *Thou shalt not steal.* Paul said, *Let him that stole steal no more...* (Ephesians 4:28). If you do not put in your full eight hours daily, you are a thief robbing your employer in a very dishonest way. If you copy another's paper at school or cheat on an exam, you are dishonest, stealing a grade in a deceitful way.

   Every ball-point pen and rubber band removed from the office is thievery. This sin must be confessed—soon! Some of you have half of the factory or office stored in the cellar or attic. After death, you will have to transport it to hell, because no thief enters heaven (see 1 Corinthians 6:10).

9. *Thou shalt not bear false witness.... These six things doth the Lord hate: yea, seven are an abomination unto him: A proud look, a LYING TONGUE, and hands that shed innocent blood, An heart that DEVISETH WICKED IMAGINATIONS, feet that be swift in running to mischief, A false witness that speaketh lies, and he that soweth discord among brethren* (Proverbs 6:16-19, emphasis mine).

   The entire listing has to do with the sins of lying and gossip. Is an eternity of separation from God worth the practice of these abominations? That is the final outcome, for outside of heaven *...are dogs, and sorcerers, and whoremongers, and murderers, and idolaters, and whosoever loveth and* *maketh a lie* (Revelation 22:15). Oh, turn from this wickedness to Christ who is *the Truth* (John 14:6).

10. The final commandment is, *Thou shalt not covet thy neighbour's house...wife, nor...any thing that is thy neighbour's.* The word *covet* means "to desire," and the world is full of desire. It is so bad, they even made a movie entitled *A Streetcar Named Desire.* Ha!

Certainly all of us have coveted at one time or another saying, "Oh, look at his big Colonial house and I have this dinky bungalow. If only I had his home." Or, "Look at the big Chrysler New Yorker he is driving and I have this Volkswagon. If only we could swap!" Or, "Look at his wife—whew! and then look at mine—ugh! If only we could switch!"

Have you ever desired anyone else's possessions? Then you have broken God's commandment. Someone resounds, "If that be true, we have all sinned." Exactly! That is why Isaiah 53:6 declares, *All we like sheep have gone astray...* and Galatians 3:22 proclaims, *But the scripture hath concluded all under sin....*

Chapter 13

Detectives for God

Multitudes trust in commandment-keeping as a means of appeasing God and entering heaven. This is drastically wrong because it leads a soul into eternal separation from God who gave the Commandments. Does this seem contradictory? It isn't when one understands God's purpose in issuing Sinai's demands. Why, then, was the first Law given?

First, because the Commandments are spiritual detectives. Now detectives accumulate evidence in order to incriminate and convict law breakers. Likewise, God's detectives, the Commandments, also incriminate and condemn the breakers of heaven's laws. In fact, they find every member of the human race guilty as an enemy of righteousness.

Proof? Romans 3:20: *Therefore by the deeds of the law there shall no flesh be justified in his sight: for by the law is the knowledge of sin.* Paul says in Romans 7:7, *I had not known sin, but by the law* [Commandments]. Romans 3:19 tells us that the Commandments were given *...that every mouth may be stopped, and all the world may become guilty before God.*

We Are All Sinners

So let's call God's policemen as witnesses and see if these things be so. Is it really true that *...all have* *sinned, and come short of the glory of God* (Romans 3:23)? There is no doubt about it! God's Commandments prove it. We listed them and explained all ten of them in the last chapter.

Have you ever broken one of these Commandments? Then you are guilty. If you egotistically, arrogantly, and proudly profess with self-righteous piousness that you have never broken one of these Commandments, you call Almighty God a liar. He said, *There is none righteous, no, not one* (Romans 3:10).

It's your word against God's. *If we say that we have not sinned, we make him a liar, and his word is not in us* (1 John 1:10). Quit fooling yourself. Let God's detectives bring you to the place of seeing your sin-laden condition. Then call upon Christ for salvation.

Do you want further proof? Then let's go back and analyze commandments six and seven. Commandment six is, *Thou shalt not kill.* First John 3:14-15 states, *We know that we have passed from death unto life, because we love the brethren. He that loveth not his brother abideth in death. Whosoever hateth his brother is a murderer: and ye know that no murderer hath eternal life abiding in him.*

Yes, hatred becomes murder in God's eyes. Surely there has been a time in every life when bitterness, animosity, and hatred toward others existed. Be honest. Have you always been a kind, gracious, loving, tenderhearted person to all people? Of course not. Then you stand convicted by God's detectives, the Commandments.

Again, commandment seven says, *Thou shalt not commit adultery.* You may think you are free from this sin because an overt act of sexual intercourse with another, outside of marriage, has never occurred. Wait a minute! Jesus said in Matthew 5:28, *...whosoever looketh on a woman to lust after her hath committed adultery with her already in his heart.* A lustful, mental longing for another becomes adultery in the sight of God.

Again you stand convicted before God's detectives if you have ever harbored impure thoughts. "Oh," you say, "I have never had an impure thought cross my mind." I have you where I want you, because you have just broken the ninth commandment, Thou shalt not lie. Every honest person knows that Satan has at some point thrown unclean images into his mental processes. This becomes sin because, *The thought of foolishness is sin...* (Proverbs 24:9).

James 2:10 goes on to say, *For whosoever shall keep the whole law* [all Ten Commandments], *and yet offend[s] in one point, he is guilty of all.* Think of it—ten-fold guilt by breaking just one point of the Ten Commandments! No wonder *...the scripture hath concluded all under sin...* (Galatians 3:22).

We Are All Condemned by the Law

God's Commandments are also declarations of doom. Romans 4:15 states, *...the law* [Commandments] *worketh wrath....* In Romans 7:10, Paul says, *...the commandment[s]...I found to be unto death.* Romans 8:2 calls the Commandments *...the law of sin and death.*

Again in 2 Corinthians 3:6, Paul says, *...the letter* [or the Law] *killeth....* Verse 7 labels the Law as *...the ministration of death* [or condemnation]. Yes, the Ten Commandments pronounce a curse on all who are not 100 percent perfect, for *Cursed is every one that continueth not in all things which are written in the book of the law to do them* (Galatians 3:10). Therefore, because of our imperfections as human beings, we all stand condemned.

Now why is the Law of God so demanding? Because it is holy and just (see Romans 7:12). So, since all have sinned and since *...the wages of sin is death...* (Romans 6:23), the Law not only uncovers our sin but also judges and condemns it. This exposure of sin through the Law is taught in Romans 7:7 where Paul says, *I had not known sin, but by the law* [by the Commandments]: *for I had not known lust, except the law had said, Thou shalt not covet.*

Then after the Law exposes sin, it also condemns the wickedness it reveals because the Law is holy in nature. Please understand this truth! It is man's sin that causes death and destruction. The Holy Law simply exposes and condemns the sin practiced by the sinner. That is the summation of Romans 7:13. *Was then that which is good* [the law] *made death unto me? God forbid. But sin, that it might appear sin, working death in me by that which is good; that sin by the* [x-ray exposure of] *commandment*[s] *might become exceeding sinful.* There it is! The Holy Law of God detects, exposes, magnifies, and finally condemns the sin that destroys the sinner.

Believers Are Not Under the Law

Finally, the Commandments are also dead decrees to the believer. Praise God! We are *...not under the law, but under grace* (Romans 6:14). A child of God is not saved by following the Commandments given to Moses. Study the Book of Galatians to further enlighten your mind to this blessed truth.

Salvation is by the grace of God, and *grace* means "unmerited favor"—yes, favor from God that hopeless sinners do not merit. It is not man's tiresome strivings that make him saved, nor is this lifetime struggle to appease God that keeps him saved. Instead, *The just shall live by faith* (Romans 1:17). *Therefore being justified by faith, we have peace with God through our Lord Jesus Christ* (Romans 5:1).

Presently, the Commandments still expose and condemn the sinner. However, once the sinner is saved through the merits of the shed blood of Christ, the Law is no longer needed. Why? Because God now lives within the believer and can deal personally with His child. I don't need a letter of instruction from my wife concerning household chores when my wife is standing by my side pointing to that which needs fixing. So it is with the saved. Romans 7:4: *...ye also are become dead to the law* [Ten Commandments] *by the body of Christ; that ye should be married to another, even to him* [Christ] *who is raised from the dead....*

In other words, now that one has the Lord, he no longer needs an instructional sheet of commandments because he has the Giver of the commandments living in his body, soul, and spirit. This is the beautiful teaching of Galatians 3:24,25: *...the law was our schoolmaster* [teacher] *to bring us unto Christ, that we might be justified by faith. But after that faith is come, we are no longer under a schoolmaster.* The teacher was needed until the day of graduation. Then his job was finished.

We see, then, that the Law was a temporary teacher pointing out right and wrong until the great Teacher would come and live in believers' hearts. At this point, His Spirit within each genuine Christian would take over the teaching position.

You don't believe it? Here is proof. Galatians 3:19: *Wherefore then serveth the law? It was added because of transgressions, till the seed should come....* What's that again? The Law was given to sinners to show them their iniquities only until the seed (Christ) should come.

Today, the Law still shows men their sins to point them to Christ. Then, as soon as He indwells the believer, the new Christian hears the voice of the Lord himself. A list of duties is no longer necessary because Christ himself does the instructing. We are also dead to the Law with respect to its damning effects because Christ has already experienced the curse of the Law in our place. Galatians 3:13 declares, *Christ hath redeemed us from the curse of the law, being made a curse for us: for it is written, Cursed is every one that hangeth on a tree.* Yes, our blessed Lord took the curse the Law had placed upon us when He died at Calvary, and those who receive Him are no longer judged or cursed (see John 3:18).

Chapter 14

The Grace of God

Salvation is a gift of God, apart from works. Anyone who rejects this statement rejects the Almighty's plan of redemption for the entire human race. There is no other way.

Is this the teaching of the Word of God? You be the judge!

Scriptural assertations pointing to salvation as a gift fill the pages of God's Word. Ephesians 2:8,9: *For by grace are ye saved through faith; and that not of yourselves: it is the gift of God: Not of works, lest any man should boast.* In Romans 5:15, we discover that the gift is by grace. Since the gift is by the grace of God, we had better define the term. *Grace* means "unmerited favor" or "favor from God that one does not deserve."

As one looks at his own sinful portrait, painted by the Holy Spirit in Romans 3, he hangs his head in shame saying, "It's true. It's true, every word of it. I deserve God's judgment because of my terrible iniquity. I do not merit His love and grace. If justice prevailed, I would be eternally separated from God, but God loved me and sent His Son to offer His blood for me at Calvary that I might have the gift of eternal life. This is truly unmerited favor, yes, favor from God that I do not deserve. Thank You, Lord."

Grace Greater Than Our Sin

This grace that is greater than all our sin is best comprehended when one studies the Holy Spirit's graphic description of every member of the human race in Romans 3:10-18. God says, *There is none righteous, no, not one... there is none that seeketh after God. They are all gone out of the way, they are together become unprofitable; there is none that doeth good, no, not one. Their throat is an open sepulchre* [or grave] *...the poison of asps* [snakes] *is under their lips: Whose mouth is full of cursing and bitterness: Their feet are swift to shed blood: Destruction and misery are in their ways: And the way of peace have they not known: There is no fear of God before their eyes.*

This horrible indictment of the human race includes you, *For all have sinned, and come short of the glory of God* (Romans 3:23). If salvation depended upon any of us, heaven would be empty. But God's grace says, "Here is a gift you do not deserve. Take it...it's yours!" This is grace, grace, marvelous grace.

When one takes the gift, receiving Christ as his personal Saviour, he immediately exchanges his rags of unrighteousness (see Isaiah 64:6) for robes of righteousness (see Isaiah 61:10). This is so because God's offer is called *the gift of righteousness* (Romans 5:17) and is in and through Christ— not human effort. Yes, *...he* [God] *hath made him* [Christ] *to be sin for us, who knew no sin; that we might be made the righteousness of God in him* (2 Corinthians 5:21). Included as a result of the gift is eternal life. What a gloriously wrapped package! Why not open it today and see the beauty of the crucified Son of God shedding His blood to save you. Then call upon His name and be saved eternally.

Does all this sound too simplistic? It shouldn't, for Romans 6:23 emphatically states that ...*the gift of God is eternal life through Jesus Christ our Lord.* Since salvation is a gift, it is wrong for any clergyman or church to preach a system of man-made works as a means of obtaining the gift. A gift ceases to be a gift if the strings of human labor are attached to it. This is what Paul had in mind in Romans 11:6 when he declared, ...*if* [salvation is] *by grace, then is it no more of works: otherwise grace is no more grace. But if it be of works, then is it no more* [a gift by] *grace: otherwise work is no more work.*

Salvation Is God's Gift

Grace and works diametrically oppose one another. It is impossible to combine them for salvation. You must choose one or the other. It is God's Word or man's. The suave-tongued oratorical genius who talks about working one's way into the Kingdom or who preaches that the Sermon on the Mount, the Golden Rule, the Ten Commandments, or obedience to the rules of the church help one in his quest for eternal life knows absolutely nothing about *the gift of God through grace.*

When one works, God becomes man's debtor, owing man spiritual wages for meritorious service rendered. Is this God's method of operation? Never! Romans 4:4,5: *Now to him that worketh is the reward not reckoned of grace* [or as a gift], *but of debt. But to him that worketh not...his faith is counted for righteousness.* Again: *Not by works of righteousness which we have done, but according to his mercy he saved us, by the washing of regeneration, and renewing of the Holy Ghost* (Titus 3:5).

Dear friend, you have nothing to do with salvation. The "good news" is that Christ died for our sins, was buried, and rose again (see 1 Corinthians 15:1-4). This "good news" is what Christ did—not what man does. Our salvation is not in the word *do* but in the word *done.*

Salvation is God's gift to wayward, hopeless, and helpless sinners. Your part is to receive the gift: *...as many as received him* [Christ], *to them gave he power to become the sons of God...* (John 1:12). The moment one receives the gift, eternal life begins and one can jubilantly shout with Paul in 2 Corinthians 9:15. *Thanks be unto God for his unspeakable gift.*

Now that God's plan has been unfolded as salvation apart from works, let's reverse the coin and consider briefly, "works, a part of salvation." Does this sound contradictory? It need not. Why? Though one is saved freely, apart from any human merit, one immediately begins to work when salvation has occurred as an evidence that Christ within is in control. Hence, Ephesians 2:10 states, *We are his* [God's] *workmanship, created in Christ Jesus unto good works....*

So, when one takes all of God's Word into account concerning "good works," he concludes that salvation is "faith plus nothing." It is all of God, and nothing man does saves or keeps him saved. Salvation is by "grace," offered freely through Christ's sacrifice, and is received by faith, apart from works. However, the bottom line demands that the received gift become effectual through a manifestation of good works.

Salvation Is Manifested Through Works

James discusses this in chapter 2:14-18. *What doth it profit, my brethren, though a man say he hath faith, and have not works? can* [this kind of] *faith save him? If a brother or sister be naked, and destitute of daily food, And one of you say unto them, Depart in peace, be ye warmed and filled; notwithstanding ye give them not those things which are needful to the body; what doth it profit? Even so faith, if it hath not works* [or does not produce works], *is dead, being alone. Yea, a man may say, Thou hast faith, and I have works: shew me thy faith without thy works, and I will shew thee my faith by my works.*

Why? Because the outflow of works is a sign that an inward faith is operative. You say, "I believe. I believe and that settles it!" It does if this belief produces love, holiness, and good works. However, a faith that is void of works is phony, for James tells us in verse 19 that the demons who eventually fill hell believe but never produce righteous acts or good works.

Friend, if all you do is quote Christianity's creeds but never display the fruit of Christianity's cross, you, too, will be lost. If one lives like the devil, acts like the devil, talks like the devil, and runs with the devil, he will eternally live with the devil. [So] *examine yourselves... [to see if you] be in the faith* (2 Corinthians 13:5).

One may know all the dogma of the faith and be able to quote great portions of the Bible, but his absence of works is indicative of a meaningless experience. *They profess that they know God; but in works they deny him, being abominable, and disobedient, and unto every good work reprobate* (Titus 1:16). God's desire is that we be *...fruitful in every good work...* (Colossians 1:10). He also wants to *...stablish...* [us] *in every good word and work* (2 Thessalonians 2:17). It will happen when one is saved.

There it is. Salvation is by grace, offered freely because of Christ's blood sacrifice. It is to be received as a gift by faith in order to have eternal life. When the "faith" transaction is made, the nature of God is imparted at "regeneration" or salvation, and this "God within" produces love, holiness, and good works.

Chapter 15

You Must Be Born Again

Forty percent of America's citizens claim to be "born again." Are they? Have they had such an experience? Are they genuinely "twice born" people? Let's see as we undertake the study of the "new birth."

John 3:1-7 states, *There was a man of the Pharisees, named Nicodemus, a ruler of the Jews: The same came to Jesus by night, and said unto him, Rabbi, we know that thou art a teacher come from God: for no man can do these miracles that thou doest, except God be with him. Jesus answered and said unto him, Verily, verily, I say unto thee, Except a man be born again, he cannot see the kingdom of God. Nicodemus saith unto him, How can a man be born when he is old? can he enter the second time into his mother's womb, and be born? Jesus answered, Verily, verily, I say unto thee, Except a man be born of water and of the Spirit, he cannot enter into the kingdom of God. That which is born of the flesh is flesh; and that which is born of the Spirit is spirit. Marvel not that I said unto thee, Ye must be born again.*

The "New Birth" Defined

Now what is this "born-again" experience? Nicodemus, a master or teacher of Israel, figured that it might have something to do with reincarnation. So he asked, *How can a man be born when he is old? can he enter the second time into his mother's womb, and be born?* Christ instantaneously refuted this reasoning by saying, *That which is born of the flesh is flesh; and that which is born of the Spirit is spirit. Marvel not that I said unto thee, Ye must be born again.*

The Greek word *anothen*, translated *again* means "from above." Thus, Christ actually said, "Nicodemus, reentrance into and rebirth from the womb of one's mother only produces a second fleshly manifestation, not a spiritual birth. For *that which is born of the flesh is flesh; and that which is born of the Spirit is spirit.* Therefore, marvel not (don't be shocked) that I said you must be born *from above*, or born spiritually."

This plain, simple, logical statement from God should "put to bed" once, for all, and forever the nonsense taught by reincarnationists. They believe that after death one is "reborn" as a human, cow, dog, or ant. (Don't step on an ant because it might *be* your **Aunt**!) Wow! If one wants to believe fairy tales, that's his business. But please do not use the Bible to propagate such heresy.

May I tell you a little story? Once upon a time, a couple believed in reincarnation. The wife, a chronic nagger, made her husband so miserable that he longingly looked forward to death. Guess what? He died. Then *she* died. He returned as a dog and *she* as a **flea**!

Quit worrying. It won't happen, McGee, because being *born again* has *nothing to do* with a fleshly conception. Neither does it have anything to do with fleshly service. That's why John 1:13, speaking about "twice-born" men, says, *Which were born, not of blood* [fleshly reproduction], *nor of the will of the flesh* [works], *nor of the will of man, BUT OF GOD.* Titus 3:5 agrees by stating, *Not by works of righteousness which we have done, but according to his mercy he saved us, by the washing of regeneration, and renewing of the Holy Ghost.*

This makes it plain that baptism, confirmation, the communion service, the Golden Rule, the Sermon on the Mount, *and* the Ten Commandments cannot save a soul. *Salvation* is of the Lord (see Jonah 2:9). That's why Romans 4:5 declares, *...to him that worketh not, but believeth on* [Christ] *that justifieth the ungodly, his faith is counted for righteousness.*

The new birth, then, is a birth into God's family, produced by the Holy Spirit, **the moment one receives Christ as his or her personal Saviour**. Let me prove this. Humans become sons or daughters by birth. Since one can only become a son or daughter by birth, it is evident that God's **SONS** and **DAUGHTERS** are **also** born into the heavenly family. This occurs as Christ is received. John 1:12 states, *But as many as received* [Christ], *to them gave he power to become the sons of God....* Christ-rejectors cannot, therefore, be sons of God. Call me bigoted and prejudiced if you will, but I simply believe the Bible. *...yea, let God be true, but every man a liar...* (Romans 3:4).

Jesus said in John 14:6, *I am the way, the truth, and the life: NO MAN cometh unto the Father, but by me.* Acts 4:12 also states, *Neither is there salvation in any other: for there is none other name under heaven given among men, whereby we must be saved.* Therefore, *...ye are all the children of God by faith in Christ Jesus* (Galatians 3:26).

How different are the teachings of God's Holy Word from the speculative guesses of men—*even clergymen*! Ordained apostates hate the teachings of the Bible. *They,* loaded with degrees (enough to give their parishioners a fever), know more than God who wrote the Book. At least it seems this way as they attempt to gain the sinner's favor by parroting the ecumenical message of the "Fatherhood of God and the Brotherhood of Man." This pleases the lost, but it is not the message found upon the pages of Holy Writ. God is not one's Father *until* a birth has occured. Blind leaders of the blind ignore this fact and distort the truth by quoting misquoted texts.

Now, taking a text out of context produces a **pretext**. This is the case as "reverends" quote the first half of Galatians 3:26. *...ye are all the children of God....* It sounds wonderful to the average pew warmer, **but is so untrue**. The **entire** verse tells the story accurately. I quote: *Ye are all the children of God BY FAITH IN CHRIST JESUS.* Christ must be received if one is to become a son or daughter. Until then, one is a child of the devil. **Ouch**! Don't blame *me* for that statement. Jesus made it in John 8:44. He said, *Ye are of your father the devil, and the lusts of your father you will do.*

The Holy Spirit also declares in 1 John 3:8, *He that committeth sin is of the devil....* We see then that one is either a child of God or a child of the devil. To become a child of God one must trust in the *shed blood of Christ* for the remission of his sins. The **moment** one makes this decision, the birth "from above" takes place and sonship begins. **Then, and only then**, can one honestly pray, [My] *Father who art in heaven, Hallowed be Thy name* (Matthew 6:9). **No man** may call God "Father" **without** this spiritual birthday.

The "New Birth" Described

One's understanding of the "new birth" or "birth from above" can be enhanced by making three brief analogies between it and the physical birth with which we are all familiar.

First, it takes a birth to live upon earth, **temporarily**. Likewise, it takes a **second birth** to live with Christ, **eternally**.

Second, one does nothing to become born physically. An act of love between man and wife produces life. Similarly, an act of love upon Calvary made eternal life a possibility for all who receive Christ.

Third, one's life upon earth begins as he is born. Likewise, eternal life begins immediately as one is "born again."

This reception of the Son of God into one's heart and life **automatically and instantaneously** makes one a child of God because John 1:12 states, *But as many as received him, to them gave he power to become the SONS OF GOD....* Spiritually speaking, then, sons are born to God as the Lord Jesus Christ is received.

This is possible only because of Christ's death and resurrection. That's what the gospel message, meaning "good news," is all about. Paul declares in 1 Corinthians 15:1-4, *Moreover, brethren, I declare unto you the GOSPEL which I preached unto you, which also ye have received, and wherein ye stand; By which also ye are saved, if ye keep in memory what I preached unto you, unless ye have believed in vain. For I delivered unto you first of all that which I also received, how that Christ died for our sins according to the scriptures; And that he was buried, and that he rose again the third day according to the scriptures.*

This is the message that **must** be accepted if one is to be "born again," "born from above," "born by the Spirit," and "born into eternal life." This gospel **must** include the proclamation of Christ's shed blood for the remission of one's sins. To bypass the blood is to destroy the message! The "good news" becomes "bad news" when the blood is omitted. One could not get to heaven by the death of Christ if Christ's decease were bloodless.

Had Christ expired via suffocation or heart attack, His death would have been in vain as far as salvation is concerned. It **had** to be death by the shedding of blood, for *...it is the blood that maketh an atonement for the soul* (Leviticus 17:11). That's why the Church was *...purchased with his own blood* (Acts 20:28), and why *...we have redemption through his blood, the forgiveness of sins, according to the riches of his grace* (Ephesians 1:7). This "good news" also tells us that *...the blood of Jesus Christ* [God's] *Son cleanseth us from all* [ALL] *SIN*

(1 John 1:7).Small wonder that 1 Peter 1:19 calls Christ's blood *precious...as of a lamb without blemish and without spot.*

This gospel message, however, is not complete without Christ's **bodily resurrection**. Permanent death would have rendered the sacrifice valueless. Therefore, Romans 4:25 states, [Christ] *was delivered* [Calvary] *for our offences and was raised again for* [or because of] *our justification.* In simpler technology, the text declares that Jehovah raised His Son from the dead to **prove** that the saved sinner's righteous standing before God was **settled forever** because of Christ's shed blood. When one accepts this gospel message as the **only way** of salvation and receives Christ who made it all possible, he **immediately** becomes a SON OF GOD. The recipient instantaneously is "born" by the Holy Spirit into the family of God and commences to celebrate his new birthday for time and eternity.

Life in a Look

Millions upon millions will be in heaven because they followed God's instructions for eternal life given in John 3:1-7. In verse seven, one is told that he must be born again and verses 14 through 16 explain God's process in performing the miracle. *And as Moses lifted up the serpent in the wilderness, even so must the Son of man be lifted up: That whosoever believeth in him should not perish, but have eternal life. For God so loved the world, that he gave his only begotten Son, that whosoever believeth in him should not perish; but have everlasting life.*

The background for this precious portion of Scripture is found in Numbers 21. The children of Israel, because of disobedience to God, had been trampling in the wilderness needlessly. Meanwhile, their constant griping got to Jehovah God, and He gave them a good spiritual spanking.

And the Lord sent fiery serpents among the people...[and many died]. *Therefore* [they] *came to Moses, and said, We have sinned, for we have spoken against the Lord, and against thee* [Moses]; *pray unto the Lord, that he take away the serpents from us. And Moses prayed for the people. And the Lord said unto Moses, Make thee a fiery serpent, and set it upon a pole: and it shall come to pass, that every one that is bitten, when he looketh upon it, shall live. And Moses made a serpent of brass, and put it upon a pole, and it came to pass, that if a serpent had bitten any man, when he beheld the serpent of brass, he lived* (Numbers 21:6-9).

What an experience! Think of it, there was **life** in a **look**! The infected victims did nothing but **obey God's message**. They came, looked, and were healed. Now John states, [Just as] *Moses lifted up the serpent in the wilderness, even so must the Son of man* [Christ] *be lifted up: That whosoever believeth in him should not perish, but have eternal life* (John 3:14-15). As there was physical life by looking at the uplifted serpent, **so there is eternal life by looking at Calvary's uplifted sacrifice.**

Since brass in Scripture depicts judgment, the brass serpent uplifted on a pole pictured judgment accomplished in behalf of the people. They only had to look and believe to live. Christ, lifted high on the cross nearly 2,000 years ago, also symbolized judgment accomplished on the part of sinners.

No doubt about it! *Christ died for our sins* (1 Corinthians 15:3). [God] *hath made* [Christ] *to be sin for US, who knew no sin; that WE might be made the righteousness of God in him* (2 Corinthians 5:21). Therefore, one need do nothing. **Christ has already been judged for the sin of all sinners.** *Just look and live, believe and be saved!* As life was imparted to the Israelites by looking, so eternal life is bestowed upon all who look and believe. It is logical, then, to conclude and theologically accurate to say that one's reception of Christ becomes the "born-again" experience, because it is this reception of the Saviour and His shed blood that makes one a "son" (see John 1:12).

The "New Birth" Is in Christ

With this background, it is easy to comprehend that "life," yea "eternal life," is **always** associated with Christ in the Scriptures. This is a necessary conclusion. Why? If one is born into God's family by receiving the Lord Jesus, then it logically follows that eternal life, **produced** by the birth, must also be in Christ. Amen and Amen!

Please put away all preconceived ideas and let God's Word speak for itself.

153

John 1:4: *In Him was life; and the life was the light of men.*

John 3:16: *For God so loved the world that he gave his only begotten Son, that whosoever believeth in him should not perish, but have everlasting life.*

John 3:36: *He that believeth on the Son hath everlasting life: and he that believeth not the Son shall not see life; but the wrath of God abideth on him.*

In John 5:40 Jesus said, *...ye will not come to me, that ye might have life.* He again declared in John 6:47, *Verily, verily, I say unto you, He that believeth on me hath everlasting life.* Hear Him in John 10:10. *The thief cometh not, but for to steal, and to kill, and to destroy: I am come that they might have life, and that they might have it more abundantly.* John 10:27,28 adds, *My sheep hear my voice, and I know them, and they follow me: And I give unto them eternal life....*

Jesus said in John 11:25,26, *I am the resurrection, and the life: he that believeth in me, though he were dead, yet shall he live: And whosoever liveth and believeth in me shall never die. Believest thou this?* Every saved heart should respond, "Yes, Lord, I believe; I believe! Thou art the eternal life, and I have been born into this unending experience. Therefore, I shall never die." Hallelujah!

Sinner, **you, too**, may experience this everlasting blessedness. John 20:30,31 states, *...many other signs truly did Jesus in the presence of his disciples, which are not written in this book: But these* *are written, that ye might believe that Jesus is the Christ, the Son of God; and that believing ye might have LIFE through his name.* I beg of you—*see it as it is*—Jesus Christ, our Lord, alone produces "eternal life," as He enters hearts.

Could anything be more obvious than 1 John 5:12? *He that hath the Son hath life; and he that hath not the Son of God hath not life.* Someone cries, "I have been baptized, confirmed, catechized, and religiously simonized and that should be sufficient." Yet, God says, *He that hath the Son hath life; and he that hath **not** the Son of God hath not life.*

Another echoes the old refrain, "I am living by the Golden Rule, the Sermon on the Mount, and the Ten Commandments. This should **insure** a reservation in heaven." Still, *He that hath the Son hath life; and he that hath not the Son of God hath not life* (1 John 5:12). The Son of God is what the new birth is all about. That's why 1 John 5:1 states, *Whosoever believeth that Jesus is the Christ is born of God....* When one is "born of God," eternal life begins because *...this life is in his Son* (1 John 5:11). **Do you know Jesus**?

The author of the Gospel of John, so frequently quoted, sums it up beautifully by saying in 1 John 5:13, *These things have I written unto you that believe on the name of the Son of God; that ye may **know** that ye have eternal life, and that ye may believe on the name of the Son of God.* You may be "born again," "born from above," "born spiritually," "born into sonship," "born into eternal life" by receiving Christ **this very moment**! Remember, it is

155

to ...*as many as* [receive] *him,* [that he gives] *power to become the SONS OF GOD, even to them that believe on his name* (John 1:12). The question is: What will **you** do with Jesus? **Neutral you cannot be.** Someday you may be asking, "What will **He** do with me?"

Chapter 16

The Necessity of the New Birth

Now that we have defined and described the new birth, we want to prove that this experience is demanded by God. Jesus said, *...ye MUST be born again* (John 3:7). He did not say that the birth was worthy of one's consideration or that one's acceptance of His proposal would be admirable. No, He said, *...ye MUST be born again.* Why?

Adamic Nature

First, we must be born from above or born again spiritually because, through our physical birth, we have inherited the Adamic nature. We are "chips off the old block." Adam, as the head of the human race, passed on the "genes" of a corrupt nature to all his posterity. Paul spells it out clearly in Romans 5:12,18,19. *Wherefore, as by one man sin entered into the world, and death by sin; and so death passed upon all men, for that all have sinned...Therefore as by the offence of one* [Adam] *judgment came upon all men to condemnation; even so by the righteousness of one* [Christ] *the free gift came upon all men unto justification of life. For as by one man's disobedience many were made sinners, so by the obedience of one shall many be made righteous.*

We conclude, then, that **every member** of the human race inherited Adam's rotten nature at birth, making each of us what our first dad was—a disobedient rebel. This old nature within us makes us lie, cheat, swear, and desire sin. *One is not a sinner because he sins. He sins because he is a sinner.*

That's what the psalmist meant in Psalm 51:5 when he said, *Behold, I was shapen in iniquity; and in sin did my mother conceive me.* The sin in this text was not sex, for, *Marriage is honourable in all, and the bed undefiled...* (Hebrews 13:4). Instead, the "iniquity" refers to the old nature formed within one at conception. This old nature contains all the germs of every known sin. That's why God declares in Psalm 58:3,4, *The wicked are estranged from the womb: they go astray as soon as they be born, speaking lies. Their poison is like the poison of a serpent....*

In the light of this convicting evidence, only rebellious sinners would say, "I don't need salvation," or "I am saved because I was born into a Christian family." God disagrees. He says, *...there is not a just man upon earth, that doeth good, and sinneth not* (Ecclesiastes 7:20). *...there is none that doeth good, no, not one* (Psalm 14:3). *All we like sheep have gone astray; we have turned every one to his own way; and the Lord hath laid on him* [Christ] *the iniquity of us all* (Isaiah 53:6). *The good man is perished out of the earth: and there is none upright among men: they all lie in wait for blood; they hunt every man his brother with a net* (Micah 7:2).

Jesus said, *...none is good, save one, that is, God* (Luke 18:19). Paul also adds a stroke on the canvas of life by stating in Romans 3:10-18: *There is none righteous, no, not one: There is none that understandeth, there is none that seeketh after God. They are all gone out of the way, they are together become unprofitable; there is none that doeth good, no, not one. Their throat is an open sepulchre* [grave]; *with their tongues they have used deceit; the poison of asps is under their lips: Whose mouth is full of cursing and bitterness: Their feet are swift to shed blood: Destruction and misery are in their ways: And the way of peace have they not known: There is no fear of God before their eyes.*

What a portrait of every member of the human race without God. Sinners possess naught but depraved natures passed on to them from generation to generation. They now need a "born-again" experience that produces a "new nature" through "regeneration." No wonder Jesus said, *...ye MUST be born again.*

Spiritual Comprehension

Secondly, the "born-again" experience is compulsory if one is to understand God. First Corinthians 2:11-14 depicts this. *For what man knoweth the things of a man, save the spirit of man which is in him? even so the things of God knoweth no man, but the Spirit of God. Now we have received, not the spirit of the world, but the spirit which is of God; that we might know the things that are freely given to us of God. Which things also we speak, not in the words which man's wisdom teacheth, but which the Holy Ghost teacheth; comparing spiritual things with spiritual. But the natural man receiveth not the things of the Spirit of God: for they are foolishness unto him: neither can he know them, because they are spiritually discerned.* **What a text! Let's dissect it.**

No man is able to understand another man *except by the human spirit commonly possessed.* This human spirit makes daily communication possible with other members of the human race. Though human beings enjoy such privileges among themselves, they are unable to conduct intelligible conversations with the *animal kingdom*, because the human spirit is missing in birds and beasts. Supposing I went into a pasture and began reading Shakespeare's *Romeo and Juliet* to Bozo the bull. What would his reaction be if I looked into his eyes and said, "Bozo, here is one of England's greatest masterpieces. Are you listening? 'Oh, Romeo, Romeo, wherefore art thou, Romeo?'" I think he might snort a little and give me a run for my money. In fact, I might fly over the fence faster than the Space Shuttle! The problem? *A communication barrier.* Now, Bozo might be the smartest bull in the herd and possess unusual qualities, but intelligible discourse would be an impossibility— *he's an animal.*

However, if a veterinarian were able to "transplant" a human spirit within the breast of the beast, communication might become a reality. Of course this is totally absurd. It could never happen.

However, by way of analogy, there is something that occurs at **conversion** which makes good "horse sense." The "new birth" allows humans to become **partakers** of God's nature (see 2 Peter 1:4). His nature enters a believer immediately as the "Great Physician" performs the miraculous transplant. Because of it, MAN, now possessing God's spirit, can, for the first time, understand God.

From this point onward he is able to grasp the truths of the Bible. The Scriptures are no longer mythological legends or contradictory pronouncements. God's Spirit, present in the "new-born" convert, makes spiritual truths unbelievably comprehensible. This is the meaning of the text which bears repeating: *...the things of God knoweth no man, but the Spirit of God. Now we have received, not the spirit of the world, but the spirit which is of God; that we might KNOW the things that are freely given to us of God. Which things also we speak, not in words which man's wisdom teacheth, but which the Holy Ghost teacheth; comparing spiritual things with spiritual* (1 Corinthians 2:11-13).

It is evident at this point that no human, regardless of I.Q., scholastic attainments, or academic degrees can by mere intelligence understand God. That's why 1 Corinthians 2:14 adds, (Get it all you college students who have been brainwashed and misled by educated pagans) *But the natural man* [or unsaved man] *receiveth not the things of the Spirit of God: for they are foolishness unto him: NEITHER CAN HE KNOW THEM, because they are spiritually discerned.*

The lost, even those with Ph.d.'s, are hopelessly incapacitated when it comes to the Bible. They have no spiritual equipment to investigate the Spirit's teachings. This takes a "supernatural" transplant by the Holy Spirit and is called the "new birth." **Then**, the believer **partakes** of the "divine nature" and God's Spirit within makes God's writing understandable. You see, one must **know** the Author of the Bible to understand the Author's writings. Until then, the Bible is as difficult and dry as Egyptian hieroglyphics to a Chinaman.

Heaven's Entrance

Third, one needs a "new-birth" experience to enter God's **presence**. Jesus said, *Verily, verily, I say unto thee, Except a man be born again, he cannot see the kingdom of God.* And again, *Except a man be born of water and of the Spirit, he cannot enter into the kingdom of God* (John 3:3 and 5).

Is it any wonder that the Saviour vehemently says in verse 7, *Ye **MUST** be born again.* None will ever see the light of the Holy City who reject Christ as personal Saviour. Instead, unbelievers and Christ-rejectors join the legion of the **doomed** *for all eternity!* Revelation 21:8 states, *But the fearful, and **UNBELIEVING**, and the abominable, and murderers, and whoremongers, and sorcerers and idolators, and all liars, shall have their part in the lake which burneth with fire and brimstone: which is the second death.*

Now do you see why *YOU MUST BE BORN AGAIN?* He who has been **born once** *dies twice,* but he who is **twice born**, *dies once*. What strange language, you say? Not really. If one is born but once—physically—he dies twice. First, the grave, then the lake of fire which is the **second death** (see Revelation 20:14). On the other hand, he who has been born twice—physically **and** spiritually—dies but once. For on such (the born again) the second death (lake of fire) **hath no power!** Will **you** die once or *twice*? Will **you** exit this earth instantly—via disease or disaster—and then enter the regions of the **doomed** forever? Why wonder? Why procrastinate? Eternity is ahead.

There is only **one way** to become spiritually born. That is *...Believe on the Lord Jesus Christ, and thou shalt be saved...* (Acts 16:31). Romans 10:13 adds, *...whosoever shall call upon the name of the Lord shall be saved.* Do it now!

Chapter 17

The Results of the New Birth

John Wesley, the founder of Methodism, repeatedly preached on the subject, "Ye must be born again." On one occasion a listener approached this servant of God and said, "Don't you know anything else except, 'Ye must be born again?'" Wesley smiled and replied, "Certainly, but the reason I preached on John 3:7, *Ye must be born again*, so often is because Jesus said, *Ye must be born again*."

Results of "The New Birth"

One can only be "born again" or "from above" if his theological concept of Christ is accurate. First John 5:1 states, *Whosoever believeth that Jesus is the Christ is born of God....* **What a power-filled statement**.

"Why?" you ask.

Because *Jesus* means "Saviour" (see Matthew 1:21) and *Christ* means "Sent One." Therefore, one must believe that the Saviour is the "Sent One" or a "born-again" experience becomes impossible. Involved in the terminology, "Sent One," is the **eternal deity** of Christ. One must believe that He *always existed*, yea was the preexistent God, the second member of the Trinity. One must believe that He was *...from everlasting* (Micah 5:2) and was "sent" to earth to inhabit a blood-filled body to die for sinners. That's why Galatians 4:4 states, *But when the fulness of the time was come* [the time for God's plan to be enacted, see Revelation 13:8], *God SENT* [not created, but **SENT**] *forth his Son....* If He sent Him, Christ preexisted, for one cannot be sent if he is nonexistent.

Now this "Sent One" came to Bethlehem's manger to die upon Calvary's tree. Yes, [He] *took upon him the form of a servant, and was made in the likeness of men: And being found in fashion as a man, he humbled himself, and became obedient unto death, even the death of the cross* (Philippians 2:7,8). No **other** Christ suffices. He **must be** the *virgin born, blood covered, resurrected God-man* or salvation is impossible. Believing this and receiving Him makes one "born of God." This in turn produces three results.

Holiness

First, the birth by the Spirit produces **holiness**. First John 3:9 declares, *Whosoever is born of God doth not commit sin; for his seed remaineth in him: and he cannot sin, because he is born of God.* Greek scholars teach that the word *commit* **should** be translated "practice." This is so because a Christian may still slip or do wrong. Believers **still** have fleshly natures *until the day of redemption*. **Then** Christ "raptures" our old "vile bodies" into His presence (see Philippians 3:20).

Presently, this **old nature** is constantly at war with the *newly produced nature* received at salvation. Paul described the battle in Romans 7 and also in Galatians 5:17. He says, *...the flesh lusteth against the Spirit, and the Spirit against the flesh: and these are contrary the one to the other: so that* [you] *cannot do the things that* [you] *would.* **However**, victory through the indwelling Spirit is *possible* for verse 16 states, *Walk in the Spirit, and* [you] *shall not fulfil the lusts of the flesh.*

It must be obvious to all Christians that there is a **constant battle** to be fought. Paul wasn't whistling in the wind when he said, *I have fought a good fight...* (2 Timothy 4:7). He knew the danger of egotistically shouting, "I could never do wrong," for he again declared in 1 Corinthians 10:12, *...let him that thinketh he standeth take heed lest he fall.*

We see, then, that it **is** possible for any child of God to commit sin but **impossible** for the *genuine* believer to live a **life** of sin. This is true because *...his seed* [the Holy Spirit] *remaineth in him: and he cannot* [practice] *sin, because he is BORN OF GOD* (1 John 3:9). When one is truly saved, Christ and the Holy Spirit enter one's heart and life simultaneously. That's right, *...if any man have not the Spirit of Christ, he is none of* [Christ's] (Romans 8:9). This blessed Spirit, living within the believer, becomes **"grieved"** (see Ephesians 4:30) and **"quenched"** (see 1 Thessalonians 5:19) when the *smallest infraction* of God's commands occurs. **The Spirit's grief, in turn, becomes the believer's heartache** as he feels what the internally dwelling Spirit experiences. This elucidates our previously discussed text which says, *Whosoever is BORN OF GOD doth not commit sin; for his seed* [the Holy

Spirit] *remaineth in him: and he cannot* [practice] *sin, because he is born of God* (1 John 3:9).

Let's go a step farther. If one is miserable over sin but **continues** to walk in disobedience to God, the offender gets a **spiritual spanking**. Hebrews 12:5-8 declares: *My son, despise not thou the chastening of the Lord, nor faint when thou art rebuked of him: For whom the Lord loveth he chasteneth, and scourgeth **EVERY SON** whom he receiveth. If ye endure chastening, God dealeth with you as with sons; for what son is he whom the father chasteneth not? But if ye be **without** chastisement, whereof **ALL** are partakers, then are ye bastards, and not sons.*

This spiritual spanking, administered to "every son" (verse 6), yea "all" disobedient "children" (verse 8), is for one purpose *and one purpose only: ...that we might be **partakers** of his **HOLINESS*** (verse 10). We see, then, that it is God's supreme desire that His children live **holy** lives. This is in accordance with their "new-birth" experience. Salvation produces holiness. Second Timothy 1:9 states, [God] *hath **SAVED** us, and **CALLED** us with an **HOLY** calling....* Again, *...God hath not called us unto uncleanness, but unto **HOLINESS*** (1 Thessalonians 4:7).

That's why Romans 6:4 states that we have been raised unto *...**NEWNESS** of life,* and why 2 Corinthians 5:17 adds, *...if **ANY MAN** be in Christ, he is a **NEW** creature: old things are passed away; behold, **ALL THINGS** are become **NEW**.* This is a *direct result* of receiving Christ. Let me explain this truth with an analogy of the physical birth.

When one is born, he receives the nature of each parent. The mixture of the genes means that both parents' traits are combined in their co-mingled product. The mean, grumpy nature comes from dad, and the "sugar and spice and everything nice" traits from mom—to hear some ladies tell it! Ha! The **combining** of the two natures within the finished product results from "human generation."

Likewise, when one is "born from above," or "born of the Spirit," he receives **God's nature** through **REGENERATION** (see Titus 3:5). As the child receives the nature of his parents through generation, the believer receives the nature of God through regeneration. This is what makes holiness possible. Since one has become a partaker of the divine nature (see 2 Peter 1:4) and since God is holy (see 2 Peter 1:16), the **nature** of God within the newly formed "babe in Christ" is divine and holy.

It certainly does not take any ingenuity to see that God within produces holy living. **HIS HOLINESS** rubs off and must be reflected in His children. The Bible commands this holiness of life through conversion: ...[you] *shall be holy; for I am holy...* (Leviticus 11:44). *...thou art an holy people unto the Lord thy God...* (Deuteronomy 7:6). They shall be called, *The holy people, The redeemed of the Lord...* (Isaiah 62:12). Paul pleads with the people of God to walk according to their standing, saying, *...yield your members servants to righteousness unto holiness* (Romans 6:19).

The apostle was concerned because he wanted all of God's people to share the joyous hour when Christ presents us holy and unblamable (see Colossians 1:22). Colossians 3:12 informs believers that they, *as the elect of God,* [are] **holy** *and* **beloved**. They are *...holy brethren...* (Hebrews 3:1). Elected to such a high calling, we are to, *Follow peace with all men, and holiness, without which no man shall see the Lord* (Hebrews 12:14). One's holy walk and talk proves that **genuine** salvation has occurred.

Strange, is it not, that denominations who push "election" the hardest are usually the cocktail-sipping, tobacco-sucking crowd. Beloved, **election** is unto **holiness**! He chose us *...in him...before the foundation of the world, that we should be* **HOLY...** (Ephesians 1:4). Preaching and teaching about "predestination" and "election" is naught but empty platitudes and vain repetition if the life of **holiness** is **missing**. In other words—pardon my grammatical error—*you ain't got it!* Why? Without holiness, **no man** shall see the Lord.

Now back to the original premise. Genuine believers may slip and fall, but they do not **remain** in the mud of sin for months and years. The Apostle John harmoniously ties the two teachings, already considered, together by saying, *If we say that we have no sin, we deceive ourselves, and the truth is not in us.* **However,** *He that* [practices] *sin is of the devil...* (1 John 1:8 and 3:8). ***Make the distinction God does, and the pieces of the puzzle fit the picture.***

In the light of what has just been discussed, let's consider the **outcome** of practicing sin. Multitudes think that walking an aisle, signing a card, and sending one's photograph for baptism constitutes a salvation experience. Soothed and salved by such religious pilgrimages to the altar or prayer room, they **continue** the practice of every abominable degradation known.

Regardless of their decadent lifestyle, all is well because once upon a time they made a beeline to the altar. Unfortunately, all they gained by it was **"exercise,"** not an **"experience."** The "move" made, the practicing sinners rest in an *unexperienced* experience and they will die as *unconverted* converts. **How deceived they are!** How **sad** they will be at the judgment when Christ cries, *I **NEVER** knew you: depart from me, ye that work iniquity* (Matthew 7:23). As I preach such convicting truth I realize that some sin-laden worldlings are angry. They are crying, "Christian liberty, Christian liberty." Ah, but *Christian liberty* is **never** a driver's license to steer one's life into the pathways of sin! Others lament, "We are under grace and thus are able to do anything and everything." Ah, but grace does **not** allow for a lifetime of disgrace! The "Apostle of grace" dogmatically teaches this.

Strange as it may seem to some, Paul's "grace" message concerning sin is identical to John's "legalistic" discourse about iniquity. Why not? God wrote all of the Bible. He used Paul, John, and others—even their personalities and vocabularies—but He **guided** *every word* into place (see 2 Peter 1:21). As a result, Paul, as well as John, makes it **clear** that one cannot **love** sin, **desire** sin, **chase** sin, **live** in sin, and check into a **sinless** heaven. Though any Christian **can** commit any sin at any time, Paul nevertheless concludes that there must be evidence of a **"new nature"** constantly **battling** against an "old nature" *if one has been born again*. **No evidence—no experience with God!** It's that simple.

This is so because the Spirit of God becomes "grieved" (see Ephesians 4:30) and "quenched" (see 1 Thessalonians 5:19) when believers sin. The believer, in turn, **shares** the grief produced by the indwelling Spirit. Then, if he **continues** in sin, he is "spanked" spiritually (see Hebrews 12:6) and may "die" prematurely (see 1 John 5:16), going home "ashamed" (see 1 John 2:28) and suffering the loss of all rewards—being saved *...as by fire* (1 Corinthians 3:15). It is foolish, therefore, to teach that Paul's "grace" proclamation allows one to live in sin.

If, at this point, one is **still** unconvinced, Paul's following warnings should settle it once, for all, and forever. Hear him in 1 Cornithians 6:9,10: *Know ye not that the unrighteous shall not* [SHALL NOT. That's right, **shall not!**] *inherit the kingdom of God? Be not deceived: neither fornicators* [premarital sex experimenters and "trial marriage" proponents], *nor idolators, nor adulterers* [extra-marital flingers and swingers], *nor effeminate, nor abusers of themselves with mankind* [homosexuals], *Nor thieves, nor covetous, nor drunkards* [social tipplers who tipple one too many], *nor revilers, nor extortioners, shall inherit the kingdom of God.*

Paul again warns in Ephesians 5:3-7: *But fornication* [premarital sex], *and all uncleanness, or covetousness* [love of materialism and filthy lucre], *let it not be once named among you, as becometh saints; Neither filthiness, nor foolish talking, nor jesting, which are not convenient: but rather giving of thanks. For this* [you] **KNOW**, *that no whoremonger* [immoral sex practitioner], *nor unclean person* [smutty jokester], *nor the covetous man, who is an idolater* [money lover], *hath any inheritance in the kingdom of Christ and of God.* [None? **None!**] *Let no man deceive you with vain words: for because of these things* [sins] *cometh the wrath of God upon the children of disobedience. Be not ye therefore partakers with them.* No doubt about it. Depraved, debauched, decadent practitioners of sin inhabit the lake of fire **for all eternity** (see Revelation 21:8).

One more judgmental alarm is sounded by Paul in Galatians 5:19-21. He says, *Now the works of the flesh are manifest, which are these; Adultery, fornication, uncleanness, lasciviousness, idolatry, witchcraft, hatred, variance, emulations, wrath, strife, seditions, heresies, envyings, murders, drunkenness, revellings, and such like: of the which I tell you before, as I have also told you in time past, that they which do such things SHALL NOT* [What? **SHALL NOT!**] *inherit the kingdom of God.* Such grammar is so simplistic and understandable that further comment is unnecessary. It all convincingly says, *He that practiceth sin is of the devil.*

Does all this mean, then, that practicing sinners have **no** hope? Perish the thought! God **loves** sinners and sent His Son to Calvary's cross to shed His blood for a **world** of wicked inhabitants. This blood, which flowed so freely from a love-filled Saviour, cleanseth from **ALL** sin (see 1 John 1:7). Because of it, a great number of Corinthians described in 1 Corinthians 6:9,10 as fornicators, idolaters, adulterers, homosexuals, thieves, covetous, drunkards, revilers, and extortioners were **eternally forgiven** as verse 11 proves. *And such were some of you: but ye are washed, but ye are sanctified, but ye are justified in the name of the Lord Jesus, and by the Spirit of our God.* This is what the "second birth" did for them and will do for **you** *today* if you receive Christ. Remember, *...whosoever shall call upon the name of the Lord shall be saved* (Romans 10:13).

Victory

The second effect of the "born-again" experience is victory. First John 5:4,5 states, *For whatsoever is born of God overcometh the world: and this is the VICTORY that overcometh the world, even our faith. Who is he that overcometh the world, but he that believeth that Jesus is the Son of God?*

Notice carefully that victory is accomplished through Christ—**not self**. Multitudes strive to overcome sin and temptation, but the flesh has no power to win the battle. The overcomer is *...he that believeth that Jesus is the Son of God. Christ in you...* (Colossians 1:27) makes the difference. He promotes the desire for victory and provides the strength.

Paul knew this well. After describing the duel of the **two natures**—the old received at birth and **new** received at conversion—he cries, *...if ye live after the flesh, ye shall die: but if ye through the* **SPIRIT** *do mortify* [put to death] *the deeds of the body, ye shall live. For as many as are* **led** *by the Spirit of God,* **they** *are the* **sons** *of God* (Romans 8:13,14). Then, having allowed God's Spirit to equip him for life's battle, he victoriously said as death approached, *I have fought a good fight, I have finished my course, I have kept the faith: Henceforth there is laid up for me a crown of righteousness, which the Lord, the righteous judge, shall give me at that day...* (2 Timothy 4:7,8).

The new nature, controlled by the Spirit, makes believers *...more than conquerors through him that loved us* (Romans 8:37). What do they conquer? First John 2:15-17 answers the question. *Love not the world, neither the things that are in the world. If any man love the world, the love of the Father is not in him. For all that is in the world, the lust of the flesh, and the lust of the eyes, and the pride of life, is not of the Father, but is of the world. And the world passeth away, and the lust thereof: but he that doeth the will of God abideth forever.* It is obvious, then, that they overcome the **world** or **worldliness** consisting of: A) the lust of the flesh, B) the lust of the eyes, and C) the pride of life. Let's consider these three items individually.

The lust of the flesh concerns itself with the cravings of one's bodily appetites. This includes illicit sex, drinking, drug addiction, smoking, or any other vice that the flesh practices. **I am not preaching perfection.** Christians can slip and fall, but that is vastly different from becoming enslaved to fleshly lusts.

The problem is not one's possession of an old nature, but the old nature's possession of a person. The latter means that one has **not** been "born again," for "regeneration" endows one with a divine nature (see 2 Peter 1:4), which immediately begins an onslaught against the old corrupt flesh. When one never experiences victory, it becomes obvious that the new nature is missing, for the "new birth" is not a new label on a defiled product but the implantation of the divine nature which changes one instantaneously. That's why 2 Corinthians 5:17 declares, *...if **any man** be in Christ, he is a **new** creature: old things are passed away; behold, **all things** are become **new**.* Enslavement to sin points to an empty profession—just lip service—and leads one into helplessness for the ages of eternity, for *...the world passeth away, and the lust thereof: but he that doeth the will of God abideth for ever* (1 John 2:17).

Where do **you** stand? Are **you** a daily "overcomer" through the power of the indwelling Spirit? **Or** are you a **slave** to lust? Remember, if there is no desire for victory, no quest for victory, no evidence of victory, there will be no victory celebration in heaven.

Next, we discover that this new nature helps one to have victory over the cravings of the **mind** through the eye gate. Lust, via the eyes, is one of the greatest promoters of immorality today. This is why pornography and abominable sex movies are destroying lives, homes, and nations. Millions presently have *...eyes full of adultery...that cannot* *cease from sin* (2 Peter 2:14). They mentally undress every woman they see and vice-versa. They purchase the latest sex magazines, hide them among their possessions, and secretly read them. They gaze at nude pictures and commit mental adultery with naked paper dolls.

Jesus said in Matthew 5:28, *...whosoever looketh on a woman to lust after her hath committed adultery with her already **IN HIS HEART***. This is what's wrong with Hollywood productions. This is why much of television's degrading influence should be opposed and stopped. Americans are becoming sex maniacs because of the manifold means created to produce excitation and lust. It is even affecting church members by the tens of thousands. Scores are walking the aisles in crusades to give up the sin which has plagued them—lustful eyes. How much farther will it go?

Once I saw a four-foot picture of a naked woman hanging in a **deacon's** garage. I asked, "Brother, aren't you a Christian and a deacon?" He meekly answered, "Yes." I pointed to his picture and said, "What's that?" He said, "Art." I said, "Art who?" **This actually happened!** Though it appears humorous now, it won't be funny later.

A day is coming when all lust-controlled sinners shall be eternally separated from God. First John 2:17 declares, *...the world passeth away, and the lust thereof: but he that doeth the will of God abideth for ever.* Is it any wonder that Romans 13:14 states, *...put ye on the Lord Jesus Christ, and make not provision for the flesh, to fulfil the lusts thereof.* And 1 Peter 2:11 warns, *...abstain* *from fleshly lusts, which war against the soul.* Someone cries, "That's easier said than done." **Not if one depends upon the indwelling Spirit rather than self!** Galatians 5:16 proves it. *Walk in the **SPIRIT**, and* [you] *shall not fulfil the lust of the flesh.*

Another area over which one may enjoy victory is one's **ego**. This has to do with haughty, arrogant boasting over one's accomplishments and gains. How often one hears church members egotistically saying, "We are now a three car family," or "We are considering the purchase of our $150,000 dream home," or "We have investments in stocks, bonds, and banks and are sitting pretty, financially."

Jesus said, *...out of the abundance of the heart the mouth speaketh* and *...by thy words thou shalt be justified, and by thy words thou shalt be condemned* (Matthew 12:34 and 37). Small wonder that James 4:4 warns, *...know ye not that the friendship of the world* [composed of the lust of the flesh, the lust of the eyes, and the pride of life] *is enmity with God? whosoever therefore will be a friend of the world is the **ENEMY*** [yes, the **ENEMY!**] *of God.* Therefore, Paul pleads in Romans 12:2, *...be not conformed to this world: but be ye transformed by the renewing of your mind....* The ways of the world lead to doom and death. **About-face for Christ!**

Love

The third and final proof has to do with **love**. First John 4:7,8 states, *Beloved, let us love one* another: *for love is of God; and every one that loveth is* **BORN OF GOD**, *and knoweth God. He that loveth not knoweth not God; for God is love.* May I repeat that? Are you listening? *This statement is so important that one's eternal existence in heaven or hell depends on it.* Hear it again. *He that* **loveth not** *knoweth not God...* (1 John 4:8).

First John 3:14 declares, *We know* [not hope, guess, or think—but **know**] *that we have passed from death unto life, because we love the* **brethren**. *He that loveth not his brother abideth in death.* The next verse says, *Whosoever hateth his brother is a murderer: and* [you] *know that no murderer hath eternal life abiding in him.* Think of it! This is astonishing. Hatred becomes murder in God's eyes, and no murderer (hater of others) has eternal life abiding in him.

A life of hate classifies one as a "child of the devil," for God says in 1 John 3:10, *In this the children of God are manifest, and the children of the devil: whosoever doeth not righteousness is not of God, neither he that loveth not his brother.* Imagine! Folks who fight, fuss, bicker, backbite, gossip, slander, malign, and criticize others are *children of the devil!* One **cannot** live a life of hate when God abides within, for *God is love.* Love is the **evidence** of one's "born-again" experience. So, *If we love one another, God dwelleth in us...* (1 John 4:12). That's why Jesus said in John 13:35, *By this shall all men know that* [you] *are my disciples,* [because] *you have* **LOVE** *one to another.*

Sad, is it not, that hate-mongers who honestly believe that bigotry, prejudice, and malice are acceptable standards for church members fill the ranks of religion. *What a shock they'll experience at the Judgment Day!* Then they'll know God meant what He said in James 1:26, *If any man among you seem to be religious, and bridleth not his tongue, but deceiveth his own heart, this man's religion is vain.*

Then they'll suffer judgment for the seven sins God hates. Perhaps these should be called the **"Seven Deadly Sins."** They are, *A proud look, a lying tongue, and hands that shed innocent blood, An heart that deviseth wicked imaginations, feet that be swift in running to mischief, A false witness that speaketh lies, and* [please get the final one] *HE THAT SOWETH DISCORD AMONG THE BRETHREN* (Proverbs 6:17-19, emphasis mine). Then when it is eternally too late, they will discover that the unrighteous, including "railers," do not inherit the kingdom of God (see 1 Corinthians 6:9).

Webster's Dictionary defines *railers* as "individuals who revile or scold in harsh, insolent, or abusive language." God help us! Our ranks are **full** of members who carry on in this manner. Through their obnoxious, hateful insolence, churches are split and souls lost. Sinner, **repent**—change your mind and ways before it is too late! You need a **"born-again"** experience! When this occurs, God's nature of **love** will become a part of you and His love will **rule** your heart.

Summary

We have concluded in this chapter that holiness, victory, and love **prove** one's salvation experience to be genuine. Where do **you** stand? Examine yourself to see whether or not you are **in the faith** (see 2 Corinthians 13:5). If the evidence is against you, *settle the issue with God immediately.* Eternity— forever and forever and forever—is a long time to be lost!

Chapter 18

This Is Christianity

It is not sufficient to simply know the terminology of the Christian faith. Knowledge about and words concerning Christ do not save a soul. Instead, *Christianity* is "Christ in you." When Christ enters one's mind, life, and heart, a change takes place. *...if any man be in Christ, he is a new creature...* (2 Corinthians 5:17).

One is neither saved nor kept by works. However, when a genuine conversion experience occurs, love, holiness, and good works are all resultant characteristics. *For we are his workmanship, created in Christ Jesus unto good works...* (Ephesians 2:10). In this chapter I want to prove that one of the evidences of salvation is *love*.

Love

I am not talking about two people becoming involved in lustful sexual activities and labeling it as true love. The words of Jesus, *Love thy neighbor as thyself,* certainly have nothing to do with immorality and wife-swapping. This would be inconsistent with His holy nature and equally illogical with His statement in Matthew 15:19, where He lumps fornication and adultery together with the vilest of sins.

He says, *...out of the heart proceed evil thoughts, murders, adulteries, fornications, thefts, false witness, blasphemies: These are the things which defile a man....* Instead He is talking about that pure, holy love which is actually God's love radiating through the life of the one in whom He dwells.

You see, when one is saved, regenerated, or born again, he immediately becomes a partaker of God's nature which includes God's attribute of love (see 2 Peter 1:4). The newly-saved individual now possesses a new nature capable of loving to the same degree that God loves. Why? It is the very nature of God transplanted within him, through the miraculous, divine operation of the Holy Spirit. His old nature could only hate, bicker, fuss, fight, fume, carp, criticize, and malign other beings. Now God's nature begins to change the past.

Don't misunderstand this simplistic truth. I am not saying that one will get into God's holy city by forcing himself to love others. But rather, the nature of God now within makes love the natural outflow of one's born-again experience. First John 4:7,8 says, *Beloved, let us love one another: for love is of God; and every one that loveth is born of God, and knoweth God. He that loveth not knoweth not God; for God is love.*

Upon the authority of this text and others I am going to dogmatically affirm that if one's heart is always full of bitterness toward others, it is undoubtedly the greatest sign that salvation is missing. Don't miss the utter simplicity of these words: *He that loveth not, knoweth not God.*

First John 3:14 states, *We know that we have passed from death unto life, because we love the brethren. He that loveth not his brother abideth in death.* Notice it does not say that the one who hates is in danger of death but that he abides in the state of death. John continues in the next verse, clarifying misunderstandings that could arise, by saying, *Whosoever hateth his brother is a murderer: and ye know that no murderer hath eternal life abiding in him.*

Friend, this is not a state of broken fellowship with the Lord. It is rather a state of damnation because no murderer, including anyone who hates his brother whom God calls a murderer, has eternal life abiding in him. Many of you reading these words today religiously carry out church functions. You say the anthems, pray the prayers, recite the creeds, give your tithes, and thank the minister for his sermons. However, you overlook the sin in your life which will doom and damn your soul in hell— the malicious hatred being harboured toward others. Get right with God. Godly love is the greatest proof one has that his experience is real.

The Love of God or Godly Love

What is godly love? How does it manifest itself? What will it produce in the lives of the saved? Let's search the Scriptures.

For God so loved the world, that he gave his only begotten Son... (John 3:16).

But God commendeth his love toward us, in that, while we were yet sinners, Christ died for us (Romans 5:8).

[Christ] *gave himself for our sins...* (Galatians 1:4).

[Christ] *loved me, and gave himself for me* (Galatians 2:20).

[Christ] *made himself of no reputation, and took upon him the form of a servant, and was made in the likeness of men: And being found in fashion as a man, he humbled himself, and became obedient unto death, even the death of the cross* (Philippians 2:7,8).

Christ also suffered for us, leaving us an example, that ye should follow his steps (1 Peter 2:21).

Hereby perceive we the love of God, because he laid down his life for us: and we ought to lay down our lives for the brethren (1 John 3:16).

Unto him [Christ] *that loved us, and washed us from our sins in his own blood* (Revelation 1:5).

Notice in these selected texts that God's love has to do with sacrifice, even to the undeserving. Yea, *while we were yet sinners, Christ died for us* (Romans 5:8). Notice again that we are to follow His steps even in dying for others. Oh, if the world could see the true love of God manifested in those who call themselves Christians, the greatest revival in history would sweep the world. It is this love that's discussed in the following texts.

But I say unto you, Love your enemies, bless them that curse you, do good to them that hate you, and pray for them which despitefully use you, and persecute you (Matthew 5:44).

Thou shalt love thy neighbor as thyself (Matthew 19:19).

The love of God makes one do for others what he would like others to do for him. This is not merely the "Golden Rule" but a command by the Lord Jesus Christ. *Greater love hath no man than this, that a man lay down his life for his friends* (John 15:13). The Christ who spoke these words fulfilled them. In further study of this subject we find that:

A. God's love radiates kindness.

Love worketh no ill to his neighbor: therefore love is the fulfilling of the law (Romans 13:10). What's the meaning of this text? The Law, called the Ten Commandments, was given by God to Moses to present to the people (see Exodus 20). The first four commandments had to do with man and God. The last six with mankind's dealings toward one another. Number five states, *Honor thy father and thy mother.* Six: *Thou shalt not kill.* Seven: *Thou shalt not commit adultery.* Eight: *Thou shalt not steal.* Nine: *Thou shalt not bear false witness* [or lie]. Ten: *Thou shalt not covet.*

Real salvation produces the nature of God within the believer. Because of it, the redeemed individual cannot continually work ill to his neighbor. He may do wrong at times because he is in a body of flesh, but he who has the nature of God within cannot—CANNOT—continually practice ill will toward his neighbor.

The divine nature does not permit one to constantly show disrespect and bitterness toward parents, does not allow one to harbour animosity and hatred toward others, does not permit one to seek sexual gratification wherever it may be found, and does not release one from being honest, trustworthy, and reliable (giving his employer a full day's work for wages paid, for example). God's love within will not produce lying in any form or manner. The practice of deceit, exaggeration, prevarication, and plain dishonesty is of Satan who is the father of lies and liars (see John 8:44). One no longer covets another's possessions but praises God for another's success. All this is so because of the emanation of God out of a saved person's life.

We also discover that:

B. God's love radiates helpfulness.

...by love serve one another. For all the law is fulfilled in one word, even in this; Thou shalt love thy neighbor as thyself (Galatians 5:13,14). The spirit of the age would make men hoard so that they have a plentiful supply of all of earth's goods, while others have little or nothing. God's love reverses man's warped sense of values. *Look not every man on his own things, but every man also on the things of others* (Philippians 2:4). In other words, see what you can do for others instead of seeking for self.

Jesus said, *It is more blessed to give than to receive* (Acts 20:35) and *Give, and it shall be given unto you...* (Luke 6:38). Christ practiced what He preached. His sacrificial heart and life made Calvary possible. Second Corinthians 8:9 beautifully tells the story. *For ye know the grace of our Lord Jesus Christ, that, though he was rich, yet for your sakes he became poor, that ye through his poverty might be rich.*

Some of you who loudly proclaim yourselves "Christians" are loaded with material blessing but you would not share any of it with the hungry brother in your church or with a destitute neighbor. Hear the Word of the Lord. James 2:14-17:

What doth it profit, my brethren, though a man say he hath faith, and have not works? can faith save him [better rendered, can this kind of faith that does nothing, be genuine salvation]? *If a brother or sister be naked* [has no clothes to wear], *and destitute of daily food, And one of you say unto them, Depart in peace, be ye warmed and filled; notwithstanding ye give them not those things which are needful* [money to buy clothes and food] *to the body; what doth it profit? Even so faith, if it hath not works, is dead....*

God's love will change one who is truly saved. He should no longer be a "Silan Marner," a "skin-flint," a "tightwad" or a religious "cheapskate."

C. Finally, God's love radiates forgiveness.

And be ye kind one to another, tenderhearted, forgiving one another, even as God for Christ's sake hath forgiven you (Ephesians 4:32). *Forbearing one another, and forgiving one another, if any man have a quarrel against any: even as Christ forgave you, so also do ye* (Colossians 3:13).

We are to forgive others as Christ forgave us. Most of us were a mess when Jesus lovingly forgave us. We were covered with vile, dirty, loathsome sins. From the soles of our feet to the tops of our heads, there was no soundness in us—only wounds, bruises, and putrifying sores (see Isaiah 1:6). We

189

had no goodness and all our righteousnesses were as filthy rags (see Isaiah 64:6).

God looked down from heaven to see if there were any that did understand and seek God. We were all together become filthy. There was none—NONE—that did good (see Psalm 14:2,3). Nevertheless, His love sent Him to die for adulterers, blasphemers, drunkards, drug addicts, extortioners, fornicators, homosexuals, killers, liars, railers, rapists, Satanists, sadists, traitors, tramps, and the rest of society's villians—because He loved us and wanted to wash us from our sins in His own blood (see Revelation 1:5).

When His earthly trial occurred, they tore His body to shreds with a Roman cat-o-nine-tails. They stuck thorns, in the form of a crown, around the flesh of His skull. They pulled His beard out by the roots and they bruised, battered, and beat His body into a mass of mutilated bleeding flesh. Still this God of love cried out from the cross, *Father, forgive them; for they know not what they do* (Luke 23:34).

Beloved, if God so loved us, we ought also to love one another (1 John 4:11). Is it possible that we humans could possess this kind of love? Stephen did. When the angry crowds crushed his head and body with rocks because of his strong preaching, he cried, *Lord, lay not this sin to their charge. And when he had said this, he fell asleep* [died] (Acts 7:60).

Oh, dear God, we are such needy people and we so desire this supernatural love that will make us forgive a man "seventy times seven," or 490 times, for the same sin. Give us Thy love in a greater measure through the Holy Spirit. Then 1 Corinthians 13:4-7 will become a reality. [Love] *suffereth long, and is kind; [love] envieth not; [love] vaunteth not itself, is not puffed up, Doth not behave itself unseemly, seeketh not her own, is not easily provoked, thinketh no evil; Rejoiceth not in iniquity, but rejoiceth in the truth; Beareth all things, believeth all things, hopeth all things, endureth all things.*

Do you have this love today? Love is the fruit of real Christianity. If you hate—you will be the loser. Those who hate are classified murderers, and no murderer has eternal life abiding in him. Is your experience with Christ real? Why not test it with God's Word.

First John 3:10: *In this the children of God are manifest, and the children of the devil: whosoever doeth not righteousness is not of God, neither he that loveth not his brother.*

If we love one another, God dwelleth in us.... If a man say, I love God, and hateth his brother, he is a liar... (1 John 4:12,20).

I have written this chapter to help some needy heart seek salvation. Animosity, bitterness, back-biting, criticism, envy, hatred, jealousy, malice, and constant railing against others indicates that there is a serious problem in one's life. The coming of the Lord is so near, and multitudes are going to be left behind. Why? They lacked one of the main evidences that their Christianity was real—the evidence of love. Do what must be done today and get your heart ready to meet the Lord.

Chapter 19

Judgment and God's Word

Five different, diversified, and distinct judgments are presented in the Bible. Men who do not rightly divide the Word of Truth (see 2 Timothy 2:15) often confuse this fact by conglomerately linking the various texts concerning judgment into one mass hodgepodge. I will not be guilty of this practice. Instead, I will differentiate and briefly describe each of the five judgments, also noting where they may be found in Scripture.

The First Judgment

Judgment number one is of the believer's sin.

Nearly 2,000 years ago, Christ came down from heaven's glory to shed His precious blood for a world of ungodly sinners. He did not die for His own sin, for He knew no sin, but became sin for us (see 2 Corinthians 5:21). Through this substitionary death—dying for you and me—all who receive this Christ can have the past, present, and future stains of sin immediately forgiven, forgotten, obliterated, and liquidated, because ...*the blood of Jesus Christ his* [God's] *Son cleanseth us from ALL sin* (1 John 1:7, emphasis mine).

As soon as the *washing of regeneration* takes place (see Titus 3:5), God cries, ...*their sins and their iniquities will I remember no more* (Hebrews

8:12). The result of being so completely washed in the blood is that, *There is therefore now no condemnation to them which are in Christ Jesus...* (Romans 8:1). This is true because Christ was already judged in the sinner's place.

Oh, what love, what compassion. Is it any wonder that Paul declares in Hebrews 2:3, *How shall we escape, if we neglect so great salvation...?*

The Second Judgment

The second judgment is of the believer's service.

This investigative probe into a believer's lifetime of works will form the basis of our present study.

The Third Judgment

The third judgment is of Israel.

During the Tribulation Hour, an enemy comes against Israel from the North (see Ezekiel 38 and 39). Then the armies of the world also converge on the Middle East (see Zechariah 14:2), and this period of bloody devastation becomes *...the time of Jacob's trouble...* (Jeremiah 30:7).

The Fourth Judgment

The fourth judgment is of the nations.

Matthew 25 pictures the return of Christ to this earth. The text correlates to and is synonymous with Revelation 19:11-16 when Christ returns to earth as *King of kings and Lord of lords.* Before He establishes His millennial Kingdom upon earth for

1,000 years (see Revelation 20:4), He purges the earth of its rebels (see Matthew 25:31-46).

The righteous are then allowed to enter God's earthly Kingdom utopia for 1,000 years and eventually, heaven for eternity. This transition is observed in 1 Corinthians 15:24-25 which states, *Then cometh the end* [Millennium]...*when he shall have put down all rule and authority and power. For he must reign, till he hath put all enemies under his feet.*

The Fifth Judgment

The fifth and final judgment is of the wicked. Commonly called "The Great Judgment Day," this solemn universal trial is described in Revelation 20:11-15: John says, *And I saw a great white throne, and him that sat on it, from whose face the earth and the heaven fled away; and there was found no place for them. And I saw the dead, small and great, stand before God; and the books were opened: and another book was opened, which is the book of life: and the dead were judged out of those things which were written in the books, according to their works.*

And the sea gave up the dead which were in it; and death and hell delivered up the dead which were in them: and they were judged every man according to their works. And death and hell were cast into the lake of fire. This is the second death. And whosoever was not found written in the book of life was cast into the lake of fire.

Friends, the hour is coming when every unsaved, unregenerate sinner must meet a Holy God for a detailed review of his life upon planet earth. When God's books are opened, every offender's tongue shall be silenced. There will be no hope then, but there is now! Why? Because Christ died for our sins (see 1 Corinthians 15:3). This means that the guiltiest of mortals can immediately be absolved by trusting in the merits of the shed blood of Jesus.

Don't procrastinate—do it today! Then you, too, will know the blessedness of John 3:18 which declares, *He that believeth on him* [Christ] *is not condemned...* because the believing are *...passed from death unto life* (John 5:24).

Chapter 20

The Resurrection of the Church

Jesus said in John 14:1-3, *Let not your heart be troubled: ye believe in God, believe also in me. In my Father's house are many mansions: if it were not so, I would have told you. I go to prepare a place for you. And if I go and prepare a place for you, I will come again....*

Paul describes this thrilling event in 1 Thessalonians 4:16,17: *For the Lord himself shall descend from heaven with a shout, with the voice of the archangel, and with the trump of God: and the dead in Christ shall rise first: Then we which are alive and remain shall be caught up together with them in the clouds, to meet the Lord in the air: and so shall we ever be with the Lord.*

Paul again says in 1 Corinthians 15:51,52, *Behold, I shew you a mystery; We shall not all sleep, but we shall all be changed, In a moment, in the twinkling of an eye, at the last trump: for the trumpet shall sound, and the dead shall be raised incorruptible, and we* [the living] *shall be changed.* This momentous event, called the "Rapture," is also described as a hope in the Word of God. The word *hope* often means a "guarantee" or an "assurance," and we will use this meaning throughout this chapter.

A Comforting Hope

First of all, the Rapture is a comforting hope or assurance. First Thessalonians 4:16,17, states that *the Lord himself shall descend from heaven with a shout, with the voice of the archangel, and with the trump of God: and the dead in Christ shall rise first: Then we which are alive and remain shall be caught up together with them in the clouds, to meet the Lord in the air: and so shall we ever be with the Lord.* It concludes by saying, in verse 18, *Wherefore comfort one another with these words.*

Let me explain this matter. What actually happens at death? The spirit, or soul, leaves the body at death. James 2:26: *For as the body without the spirit is dead....* Where does that spirit go? The blessed Holy Spirit, through the Apostle Paul, answers this question in 2 Corinthians 5:6-8.

I want you to read these verses carefully because there are those who teach that the soul, or spirit, stays in the body until the resurrection. I think these verses refute that belief. *Therefore we are always confident, knowing that, whilst we are at home in the body, we are absent from the Lord: (For we walk by faith, not by sight:) We are confident, I say, and willing rather to be absent from the body, and to be present with the Lord.*

The soul does not sleep in the body until the resurrection. Were this true, there would never be a time when the spirit and soul are absent from the body. They would continually remain together until the resurrection of the dead. But Paul says there is a time when it is absent from the body, for he says, *to be absent from the body* [is] *to be present with the Lord.*

The argument of the apostle is abundantly clear in Philippians 1:21-24. *For to me to live is Christ, and to die is gain.* Why, if you are going to lie around in the grave until the resurrection? Why is it gain to die? Paul answers these questions in the following verses. *But if I live in the flesh, this is the fruit of my labour: yet what I shall choose I wot not. For I am in a strait betwixt two....*

Or in modern English, "I am having difficulty in deciding between two alternatives: Number one, to depart (die) and to be with Christ, which is far better." Sleeping in the ground for hundreds of years? No! To depart and to be with Christ, which is far better. Or number two, to abide in the flesh (the body) is more needful for you." Paul said, "If I die, I can go home with and be with Jesus. If I live, I can preach the gospel."

Now if Paul knew that he was going to be in the ground for the next two thousand or three thousand years, he would have said, "God, since I will know nothing when I am dead, let me live to be three hundred years of age, if possible, so I can preach." That is not his argument here. His argument is, "If I depart, I can go and be with Jesus. If I remain, I can preach the gospel. Because I want to be with Jesus and because I want to preach, I have a difficult time deciding between the two." Those who advocate the doctrine of unconsciousness until the resurrection avoid these portions of Scripture.

Paul desired the Rapture simply because he then would not become an uncovered soul, a soul which goes to heaven without a body. Look at 2 Corinthians 5. He says, *For we know that if our earthly house of this tabernacle* [this body] *were dissolved, we have a building of God, an house not made with hands, eternal in the heavens. For in this we groan, earnestly desiring to be clothed upon with our house which is from heaven* (verses 1,2).

Or, in plain English, "I would desire the coming of the Lord so as to receive the new covering for my soul." Verse 3: *If so be that being clothed* [with this new body] *we shall not be found naked,* or, have a soul that has no bodily covering, which happens when one goes to heaven prior to the Rapture.

Verse 4: *For we that are in this tabernacle do groan, being burdened: not for that we would be unclothed* [go to heaven without a body], *but clothed upon* [receive the new covering for the body]. So there is a time in heaven when God's people are in the Lord's presence as spirits just as God is a Spirit (see John 4:24).

Does this mean that we will not be able to recognize one another in a spirit form? No. We in this world have physical eyes, but in the next world will have spiritual eyes. You say, "How do you know that?" Because Jesus was a Spirit before He came to earth in a body with blood to die on the cross.

Proof? Philippians 2:5: *Let this mind be in you, which was also in Christ Jesus: Who, being in the form of God....* Form. It is probably not as great as having our own body. Nevertheless, when we leave this body—*absent from the body...present with the Lord*—we get this new form, and we remain in that form until Jesus calls at the time of the Rapture. Then our bodies go into His presence.

The first coming of Jesus Christ saves the soul. The second coming of Jesus Christ saves the body. Let me prove this. First Thessalonians 4:14 says that when Christ returns He brings the dead with Him, those that sleep in Jesus. Verse 16 says that He comes for the dead. How can He bring the dead with Him (verse 14) and still come for the dead (verse 16)?

The part He brings with Him is that part which left the body at death. The part that He comes to get is that part which is in the grave, the body. Then body, soul, and spirit, we sweep through the heavenlies to meet our loved ones, to wrap our arms around one another, and to be reunited, bodily.

The glorious thought is that at death we go to glory without our bodies and become spirit beings like the Father and Holy Spirit. At the Rapture—the comforting hope—our spirits are reunited with our bodies, and there in that great assembly in heaven we meet our loved ones again in bodily form. Though we may not comprehend every detail, yet it is thrilling to know that we will be with our loved ones who have gone on before and are with Jesus.

We sing the song, "Friends will be there I have loved long ago; Joy like a river around me will flow; Yet, just a smile from my Saviour, I know, Will through the ages be glory for me." The greatest thing is that we shall see His face (see Revelation 22:4).

A Blessed Hope

Second, the promise of Christ's return for His own at the Rapture is a blessed hope or assurance. Titus 2:13 says, *Looking for that blessed hope, and the glorious appearing of the great God and our Saviour Jesus Christ.* It is blessed because we shall miss the Tribulation.

A horrible time of judgment is coming upon this earth soon. Jesus predicted a time of violent revolution in Matthew 24:37: *But as the days of Noe* [Noah] *were, so shall also the coming of the Son of man be.* How was it in Noah's day? Genesis 6:11: *The earth was filled with violence.*

In Luke 21:25, Jesus said that upon the earth shall be *distress of nations, with perplexity.* The word *perplexity* means "nations in trouble with no way out," and certainly this is the picture of the hour.

Soon terrible judgment—catastrophic, cataclysmic, and convulsive—will fall upon the earth. First, however, the greatest evacuation in history, the out-calling of the Church, will precede this period of calamity. This is certainly a blessed hope! Amen.

Rexella and I recently stood in the Valley of Megiddo, where the Battle of Armageddon is to be fought. We remembered that the blood will flow to the bridles of the horses for a distance of 200 miles, the exact length of the Holy Land (see Revelation 14:20). Praise God, seven years prior to its occurrence, we will be gone, and that is a blessed hope.

News commentators have warned of a rapidly approaching hour of famine. Revelation 6:8 depicts the time. *And I looked, and behold a pale horse: and his name that sat on him was Death, and Hell followed with him. And power was given unto them over the fourth part of the earth, to kill with sword, and with hunger, and with death, and with the beasts of the earth.*

Revelation 14:11 goes on to say, *And smoke of their torment ascendeth up for ever and ever: and they have no rest day or night, who worship the beast* [or Antichrist] *and his image, and whosoever receiveth the mark of his name* [666]. (Order my book *11:59...and Counting!* for a full explanation of the number 666.)

What a nightmare of blackness and darkness is going to sweep over this earth! Men will long to die and will say to the mountains and rocks, *Fall on us, and hide us from the face of him that sitteth on the throne, and from the wrath of the Lamb: For the great day of His wrath is come...* (Revelation 6:16,17).

Notice that this time is called *the great day of his* [God's] *wrath* and that it is sent upon a wicked, sin-debauched world because mankind refuses to repent (see Revelation 9:20). In 1 Thessalonians 5:9 however, we find that *God hath not appointed us* [His children] *to wrath....* There is that word again. It is the wrath just mentioned, the Tribulation Hour and not hell, and we are delivered from it.

What a blessed hope! We are going home soon, before this hour of conflagration begins. Revelation 3:10: *Because thou hast kept the word of my patience, I also will keep thee from the hour of temptation, which shall come upon all the world, to try them that dwell upon the earth.*

The judgments begin in Revelation 6, but the Christians are evacuated, raptured, snatched away—yea lifted up and out—before the calamity starts. How do I know? Because in Revelation 4:1 John hears the *Come up hither* invitation. He says, *After this I looked, and, behold, a door was opened in heaven: and the first voice which I heard was as it were of a trumpet talking with me; which said, Come up hither, and I will shew thee things which must be* [or come] *hereafter.* As believers we are shown the judgments of chapters 6-19 in the Book of Revelation from the heavenly home.

Many have sent me booklets debating these things, talking about post-Tribulationism. Well, if they want to preach that people are going through this final blitzkrieg on earth that is their prerogative. I am going to preach the blessed hope that we are going home soon, before earth's bombardment begins. I believe that the Bride of Christ will be spared, and I am personally looking forward to the honeymoon in glory with Jesus, rather than the seduction of the Antichrist.

A Purifying Hope

Third, the Rapture is a purifying hope or assurance. First John 3:2,3 states, *Beloved, now are we the sons of God, and it doth not yet appear what we shall be: but we know that, when he shall appear, we shall be like him; for we shall see him as he is. And every man that hath this hope in him purifieth himself, even as he is pure.*

Books on the return of Christ are now best-sellers. I praise God that it is so. *666* by Salem Kirban, *The Late Great Planet Earth* by Hal Lindsey, and *Things to Come* by Dr. Dwight Pentecost are a few of the better known volumes on this eschatological truth. Thank God for every man who is warning the human race. Praise the Lord for every preacher who is proclaiming this truth.

However, the disturbing thing to me is that in the midst of the greatest prophetical bombardment in history, Christians are still dead—in all denominations. Generally this is true because we are hearers of the Word and not doers (see James 1:22). God looked ahead and told us this condition would prevail. Because of it, we know that we are in the last hours before His return. Revelation 3:15,16 pictures the Laodicean Church—cold, dead, lukewarm, prior to the Lord's return. *I know thy works, that thou art neither cold nor hot: I would thou wert cold or hot. So then because thou art lukewarm, and neither cold nor hot, I will spue thee out of my mouth.*

Though the Church is lukewarm, individually this does not have to be so. Many believers who will read this book say they know all about prophecy. They claim to know who the Antichrist will be and even the number of hairs on his beard. Let's quit quibbling! I do not set myself up as the final authority. We will all have a lot to learn when we get to glory and sit at the feet of Jesus.

The one thing that we should all learn at this point—whether we believe in the pre- or post-Tribulation Rapture—is that Jesus Christ is coming soon, and when He returns He will either be our Saviour or our Judge! If we really believe, we should allow it to become a purifying message in our lives. Let's get out of the dance halls and movie theaters. Let's get rock music out of our lives. Let's throw away the cigarettes and cigars. Some folks are all wrapped up in promiscuity and uncleanness. They like dirty magazines. Others swear, fight, and gossip. Still, many of them sit in the churches and talk about Christ and even talk about the coming of the Lord. I do not believe they really know what it is all about, for when one really knows it and really believes it, his life will be changed. You cannot get into heaven with all of your filthiness.

Revelation 21:27 says, *And there shall in no wise enter into it* [heaven] any thing that defileth.... You have to get washed in the blood of Jesus Christ and then keep the picture of the coming of the Lord before your eyes daily and let it purify your life.

Christian, does the Lord Jesus Christ have first place in your life? Are you living for Him daily, walking in the Spirit (see Galatians 5:16), and doing those things that are pleasing in His sight (see 1 John 3:22)? Are you ready for God's investigative judgment of your lifetime of love and service at the Judgment Seat of Christ (see 2 Corinthians 5:10)? Oh, the promise of Christ's return is a comforting, blessed, and purifying hope. Make it your hope today!

Other Books by Jack Van Impe

Heart Disease in Christ's Body

Shocking! Explosive! Documented! A ringing defense of historic, biblical Fundamentalism and a call for love and cooperation among all members of the body of Christ.

328 pages $6.95

11:59...and Counting!

What does the future hold for you and your loved ones? The questions that plague humanity are answered in this detailed account of mankind's march toward the Tribulation, Armageddon, and the hour of Christ's return.

324 pages $6.95

Israel's Final Holocaust

Over 218,000 in print! One of the most helpful explanations of Israel's role in end-time Bible prophecies ever published. What will the final holocaust be...and how will it affect you? $4.95

ALCOHOL: The Beloved Enemy

Liquor and the Bible. Filled with wisdom and reasoning, this important book thoroughly covers the alcohol question. Includes historic background, current research, and statistics that may shock you. Bible help for a major problem. $4.95

Revelation Revealed

Yes, you *can* understand what many consider to be the most complex book in the Bible. Dr. Van Impe's verse-by-verse teaching reveals the meaning of this prophetic treasure. $4.95

The Baptism of the Holy Spirit

Dr. Van Impe's easy-to-understand study of who the Holy Spirit is, what He does, and why His baptism is for every believer. Includes what the Bible says about the personality, attributes, gifts, fruit, and power of the Holy Spirit. $1.95

God! I'm Suffering, Are You Listening?

Why do good people go through seemingly senseless suffering? Dr. Van Impe explains from a biblical perspective why even Christians suffer and the best way to make the most of misfortune. $1.95

The Happy Home: Child Rearing

Many parents are confused about how to raise their children to love and serve God. Dr. Van Impe provides sound Bible principles, as well as practical advice for raising children to be happy Christian adults. $1.95

America, Israel, Russia, and World War III

What will the end of the world be? Is a nuclear holocaust inevitable? Dr. Van Impe explains how Bible prophecy is being fulfilled, and the roles America, Israel, and Russia will play in the Battle of Armageddon. $1.95

Escape the Second Death

Five powerful salvation messages especially directed to the unsaved. A great witness tool. Explains the Bible way to be born again. (Excerpted from *Great Salvation Themes*.) $1.95

Exorcism and the Spirit World

What every Christian should know about Satan, demons, and demonic activity. Reveals the dangers of association with the occult, describes Satan worship, and tells how to defeat demon forces through the delivering power of the Holy Spirit. $1.95

Order from: Jack Van Impe Ministries
Box J • Royal Oak, Michigan 48068
In Canada: Box 1717, Postal Station A,
Windsor, Ontario N9A 6Y1

JACK VAN IMPE MINISTRIES
ORDER FORM

QTY	DESCRIPTION	PRICE EACH	TOTAL
	HEART DISEASE IN CHRIST'S BODY	$6.95	
	11:59... AND COUNTING!	$6.95	
	ISRAEL'S FINAL HOLOCAUST	$4.95	
	ALCOHOL: THE BELOVED ENEMY	$4.95	
	REVELATION REVEALED	$4.95	
	GREAT SALVATION THEMES	$4.95	
	THE BAPTISM OF THE HOLY SPIRIT	$1.95	
	GOD! I'M SUFFERING, ARE YOU LISTENING?	$1.95	
	AMERICA, ISRAEL, RUSSIA, AND WORLD WAR III	$1.95	
	THE HAPPY HOME: CHILD REARING	$1.95	
	ESCAPE THE SECOND DEATH	$1.95	
	EXORCISM AND THE SPIRIT WORLD	$1.95	

TOTAL AMOUNT ENCLOSED

NAME _____

ADDRESS _____

CITY _____STATE _____ZIP _____

Please tear out Order Form and send to:
  Jack Van Impe Ministries
  Box J • Royal Oak, Michigan 48068
  In Canada: Box 1717, Postal Station A
  Windsor, Ontario N9A 6Y1